Abductive Analysis

Iddo Tavory and Stefan Timmermans

ABDUCTIVE ANALYSIS
Theorizing Qualitative Research

The University of Chicago Press · Chicago and London

Iddo Tavory is assistant professor of sociology
at New York University. **Stefan Timmermans** is
professor of sociology at the University of California,
Los Angeles. He is the author of *Postmortem: How
Medical Examiners Explain Suspicious Death* and
coauthor of *Saving Babies? The Consequences of
Newborn Genetic Screening*, both published by the
University of Chicago Press.

The University of Chicago Press, Chicago 60637
The University of Chicago Press, Ltd., London
© 2014 by The University of Chicago
All rights reserved. Published 2014.
Printed in the United States of America

23 22 21 20 19 18 17 16 15 14   1 2 3 4 5

ISBN-13: 978-0-226-18028-1 (cloth)
ISBN-13: 978-0-226-18031-1 (paper)
ISBN-13: 978-0-226-18045-8 (e-book)
DOI: 10.7208/chicago/9780226180311.001.0001

Library of Congress Cataloging-in-Publication Data
Tavory, Iddo, author.
Abductive analysis : theorizing qualitative research /
Iddo Tavory and Stefan Timmermans.
pages ; cm
Includes bibliographical references and index.
ISBN 978-0-226-18028-1 (cloth : alk. paper) —
ISBN 978-0-226-18031-1 (pbk. : alk. paper) —
ISBN 978-0-226-18045-8 (e-book)
1. Abduction (Logic) 2. Qualitative research.
3. Science—Methodology. I. Timmermans, Stefan,
1968– author. II. Title.
Q175.32.A24T38 2014
511.3′1—dc23

                                    2014011271

CONTENTS

INTRODUCTION: TOWARD ABDUCTIVE ANALYSIS

Qualitative researchers navigate treacherous waters. On the starboard side lurks an overly descriptive account. The researcher gathers detailed narratives of people doing things, orders them according to broad themes, and lets the data speak for itself. Manuscripts by authors who succumb to this temptation are easily recognizable by long data excerpts interspersed with a few summary sentences that capture the gist of what the reader should pay attention to. Often the rudimentary taxonomy is preceded by a quick, almost embarrassed, venture into contemporary theory that has little relevance to the data presented. Such manuscripts may be highly readable, if only because social worlds we know little about are inherently interesting. But they mostly satisfy the voyeur in us. To the extent that we get anything theoretically out of the text, it fits the Balinese adage "Other fields, other grasshoppers."[1]

In all too many circumstances, such researchers are so unsure of how to think theoretically about their work that their research does not reach publication. Archival materials, painstakingly gathered interview tapes, and hundreds of pages of observations are diligently coded and then tucked away in boxes. Computer files with neatly listed transcripts and field notes are dutifully copied whenever the researcher upgrades computers, but are no longer accessed. The research project is left unfinished, and the researcher hangs on to the faint hope that a future self, colleague, or student will take it on.

Equally problematic is the danger on the port side. The researcher aims to fit ideas into a predetermined theoretical account, usually developed by some *en vogue* theorist. Here the research serves either as a contemporary illustration of or, at best, a minimal twist on the account the great theorist has set out. When it is done well, there is an art to such writing, which integrates data snippets with dense theoretical exegesis. Yet in many cases, researchers achieve these theorizations at the expense of paying much attention to their own observations. These researchers are so wedded to a conceptual framework that all they do is repeat or add a minor nuance to their preferred theory. The frameworks are powerful currents in heavily travelled shipping lanes, in which every attempt at a different route ends in a drift back toward a well-known destination.

Following these currents may facilitate writing and publication, as they are the path of least resistance. But they also act as powerful blinders—they push us to ignore many of the surprises that emerge during fieldwork, to dismiss as noise any observation that does not fit predetermined conceptual categories. Reading such work, we often squirm in discomfort. The data is thin and doesn't quite fit the theorization. We have a distinct feeling that the observations were a bothersome hiccup on the way to a generalization. Sometimes we wonder why the authors even took the trouble to do the empirical work; it seems they knew what they would find, and the theory seems to have said it all before.

Both of these approaches fall short of the promise of qualitative research. A better course would be to develop a double story: one part empirical observations of a social world, the other part a set of theoretical propositions. In good research, these two parts of the story not only intertwine but amplify each other. The theoretical account allows us to see things in the empirical that we would gloss over. The empirical description, in turn, pushes the theorization in unexpected directions.

Balancing theory and observations is a particularly vexing problem in qualitative work. The starting costs are relatively low—a trip to the archives, a small transcription budget, or simply time to do observations. The venture seems to be immediately rewarding. A mountain of data quickly grows, allowing the researcher to describe the complexity of a particular social world. But as the data piles up, the researcher's attempt to theorize it requires stripping away some empirical complexity.[2] The messiness of social life that makes qualitative research so attractive renders the construction of theories difficult. Theories emerge out of the double movement of reducing data and extending it to other sites, other phenomena, and other potential research subjects. At some point the qualitative researcher realizes with frustration that conceptualization and theory construction requires letting go of parts of the empirical story. Descriptive and pretheorized accounts are intended as strategies to assuage the anxiety and even guilt associated with such a reduction of the richness of observation. And yet the pitfalls of these accounts only compound such anxieties.

Although this uneasy relationship among observations, method, and theory construction remains one of the key dilemmas facing any qualitative researcher, relatively few resources are available for addressing it. Most writers on the theory of method aim to shore up the qualitative researcher's methodological credentials, rather than to think through the relationship among data, method, and theory. With the exceptions of the inductive and deductive approaches we outline below, the best books taking this problem as their starting point are organized as a set of heuristics, or tricks of the trade that researchers can use as a way to get themselves out of an intellectual rut in the process of their research.[3]

The reason for this neglect is historical. In the mid- and late twentieth century, qualitative research was juxtaposed to quantitative research, which had made great methodological strides in its sophistication and reach. In response to their increasing marginalization, qualitative researchers (at least in American academia) spent much of their intellectual energy boosting their methodological credentials. After all, stripped of its methodological dress-up, participant observation looks a lot like hanging out with people, and interviewing like a way to say the researchers had a few conversations. How can such mundane methods compete with inferences based on statistical analysis? The response beginning in the 1960s was to formalize observation and interviewing as methods. The code word for early attempts at methodologizing qualitative research was *rigorous*. In order to buttress their position, researchers formalized qualitative methods, articulating specific evaluation criteria, methodological steps, and epistemological positions. Thus we saw the emergence of a naturalistic paradigm in contrast to the positivism associated with quantitative methods and natural sciences,[4] and a focus on coding technologies in qualitative research.[5]

In recent years, the marginalization of qualitative research has abated somewhat,[6] and the gravity of methodological scholarship has shifted toward internal discussions about the merit and quality of qualitative research. Across disciplines, researchers have discussed the implications of postmodernism for qualitative researchers' grounds for representation and authority,[7] but have also given more attention to the relation between theory and observation. Research in both urban ethnography and cultural anthropology has come under fire in heated published debates that have a strong moral streak.[8] One fundamental issue running through these debates is precisely this relation between observation and theorization.

The relation among theory, observation, and method thus remains an Achilles heel of qualitative research. Yet the circumstances are different from those of the 1960s, when the rigor wave started rolling in. The key challenge is not to justify the scientific character of qualitative methodology or to provide quick heuristic fixes, but to rethink what it means to collect and interpret data with an eye on theory construction.

Of course, both inductive and more deductive approaches to qualitative research have already sketched pathways to theory construction. The current standard approach to theoretical conceptualization is grounded theory, an inductive data analysis methodology developed in the late 1960s. Although we remain sympathetic to the methodological steps developed by grounded theorists, and although we adopt some of them, we—and many others—are convinced that the inductive legacy of grounded theory has thwarted rather than aided theory construction. Time and time again, practitioners find themselves stranded on the shores of tedious description, and precious few novel theoretical accounts have come out of the grounded theory tradition.

An alternative approach to the relationship between theorization and observation is a family of deductive methods, particularly the extended case method,[9] which has gained momentum because it has assured researchers that it will deliver them to the promised land of theoretical sophistication and moral relevance. Yet whereas grounded theory flounders in endless description and minimal conceptualization, this more deductive approach often finds itself stranded on the opposite shore. Researchers design their studies around a set of comparisons that make sense only under a priori theoretical assumptions, and they often find that their comparisons are thin, uninteresting, and unsuitable to the experiences they encounter. So they tend to ignore their data or cut it up in little snippets, then focus on reiterating (or, at best, slightly modifying) an existing theory.

The pitfalls of both inductive and deductive approaches are not incidental. Although practitioners in both camps often admit in private conversations that their actual practice is more flexible than their methodological admonitions, their conception of the relation between theory and observation seeps into their research design and the writings they produce. The theory of method embedded in these approaches constitutes a set of heuristic maps. And it is on this account that they so often fail.[10]

Abductive Analysis: The Research Context

This book aims to serve as an alternative navigational map for constructing empirically based theorizations. It provides a way to think about research, methods, and theories that nurtures theory construction without locking it into predefined conceptual boxes. We offer an account of the relationship among observation, theory, and method that is grounded in pragmatist philosophy. Inspired by early American pragmatism, and especially the work of Charles S. Peirce, we view research as recursively moving back and forth between a set of observations and a theoretical generalization. The act of analyzing data requires that we pitch our observations in relation to other potential cases, both within and outside of our field. As these potential cases are then checked against other experiences, we amend them and generalize anew, thereby creating more potentials, ad infinitum. The fundamental question organizing all data analysis—"What is this data a case of?"—is a semiotic question: a question of the ongoing construction of meaning. Theorization in a pragmatist key is a continuous movement between potentials, actualizations, and generalizations. This movement back and forth between theoretical generalization and specific data brimming with potential participates in an ongoing intellectual conversation.[11]

The core idea of Peirce's pragmatism that we develop is the notion of abduction, which inspires the name for our approach: abductive analysis. For now it is sufficient to understand abduction in relationship to induction and deduction. Induction refers to the process of collecting new data and using it to strengthen or problematize well-established theories. Deduction, on the other hand, suggests a hypothesis about specific observations that is already based on existing theory. As Peirce noted, neither induction nor deduction is particularly creative, because neither leads to new theories. Theory generation requires us to move away from our preconceived notions and to create new narratives about the phenomenon we are trying to explain. Abduction occurs when we encounter observations that do not neatly fit existing theories and we find ourselves speculating about what the data plausibly could be a case of. Abduction thus refers to a creative inferential process aimed at producing new hypotheses and theories based on surprising research evidence. Abduction produces a new hypothesis for which we then need to gather more observations.

The challenge in appropriating a pragmatist approach and Peirce's notion of abduction for qualitative data analysis is to translate what may be seen as a vague prescription—"Be creative!"—into research practice and design. How do we create an environment conducive to the discovery and explanation of unexpected findings? We begin the book by stressing two aspects of this challenge: the role of in-depth familiarity with a broad variety of existing theories and the role of close attention to methodological steps that help us notice observations and draw out conceptual dimensions.

Although this may seem a pretty commonsense way to start thinking, these prerequisites constitute a rupture with existing approaches to data analysis. In-depth knowledge of a broad variety of theories breaks with the inductive approach of grounded theory, which privileges the emergence of theoretical insights out of data that are mythically unencumbered with theoretical preconceptions.[12] It also, more surprisingly, breaks with deductive approaches that seem to assume that we come to our study armed with only one theory at a time. And although deductive researchers often do good methodological work, they are so wedded to the idea that we come to the field already theorized that they sideline the importance of methodological steps to theory construction.

Believing that one can construct theory within a research context presumes a specific epistemological position on research and theory. Drawing on the work of Hans Reichenbach and Karl Popper, much twentieth-century philosophy of science created a firewall between the context of discovery and the context of justification of scientific theories. These philosophers did not delve too deeply into the discovery of theories, relegating such discovery to a side project for "empirical psychology."[13] Instead, they drew attention to the logic of justification. How do we know that a scientific theory is true, or at least "true until further notice," once it has been formulated? Much of the debate between Karl Popper and the logical positivists, for example, revolved around these demarcation criteria in the context of justification. Are theories verifiable? Or, on the contrary, is a good scientific theory one that can be empirically falsified?

One of Peirce's important contributions to the philosophy of science is his refusal of the distinction between discovery and justification. Instead, Peirce argued that creativity is inherent in the research process. If his semiotics and notion of abduction are to be taken seriously, any division of labor between creativity and the rigorous checking of theories against observations is empirically wrong: researchers theorize on the go. The discovery-justification division is also analytically wrong. When scientific work is artificially divided into these two realms, theorization becomes mystical: a flash of genius that defies explanation. And by extension it becomes something that great others can do, but not us mortals. Letting go of this myth allows us to appreciate that there is a unified context of research within which discovery and justification are inseparable moments.

This view also implies a specific position about the role of theories: without reducing theorization to a mechanized process, it suggests that theory production is a craft, something that we can become better at by being part of a community. Notions of evidence and of generalization are tied to methodological standards and available theorizations located in an intellectual social world—whether the world is that of sociology, nursing, political science, anthropology, or organizational theory, or crosses traditional academic disciplines.[14] The craft of theorizing in the research act is then to learn how to solve a practical problem: making sense of data.

The Thrill of Qualitative Research

The pragmatist approach we develop has important advantages. Abductive analysis provides us with a coherent epistemological position that is centered on the relationship among theory, method, and observation. Because epistemology infuses research design, this approach helps us craft stronger research. Spelling out the general position, abductive analysis provides purchase on specific aspects of the research context that are often mystified in qualitative research. Abductive analysis thus outlines the construction of causal accounts and their limitations; the relation among forms of variation, observation, and theorization; the uneasy relationship between explanations and categories used within the field as compared to the categories used by social scientists; and much more. Thus our approach provides guidelines for the construction and evaluation of key steps in the research act.

A pragmatist approach also helps us to address an existential question: Why do we do qualitative research at all? We began writing this book for many reasons, but one key impetus was that we felt that current approaches to the relation among theory, method, and observations often sap the joy from social research. There are many warrants for conducting qualitative research—from the aspiration to shape public opinion, to a desire to capture and document a fleeting form of social life, to an interest in crafting a theory that transcends time and place, to simple voyeurism. There are also many ways to go about theorizing. Whatever the warrant and whatever the theoretical resources the researchers draw upon, one of the seductions of qualitative research is the sense of intellectual adventure.

The thrill of research resides precisely in the way in which we muddle through and puzzle out aspects of our research project.[15] We come in with possible ideas, and we quickly become disillusioned with our preconceptions and fascinated by all the ways in which the field operates "all wrong." We return to the theory, and back to the field, and slowly piece together a theoretical account that can explain our observations, potentially illuminating a broader point that we couldn't have even guessed at when we began our work. Time and again, we have discovered that the observations and patterns we find in our research projects surpass anything we could have imagined about the field, and that the theorization we end up with is more interesting than what we could have dreamed up within the convenient confines of our office.

Whatever other reasons motivate our research, this excitement allows us to stick to it, to spend months and years poring over observations and looking for diverse sources of inspiration through which to theorize it. This excitement does not emerge automatically. To experience it, we must organize the research project in particular ways. Neither the reification of methods in grounded theory nor a focus on one's favorite theory in extended case method does justice to this excitement. We have spoken to grounded theory practitioners who were dutifully coding mountains of data with no end in sight, and deductive researchers who were mildly annoyed by the fact that it took so long to get interviewees to come out with "the right quote." Abductive analysis is an attempt to both do justice to the process of theorizing and to revive the excitement of discovery in qualitative work.

1: THE ALTERNATIVES

Where does a researcher turn to analyze qualitative data? Countless how-to books and software programs adapt qualitative data analysis to specific academic disciplines.[1] Virtually all of those tools attempt to lead to a thematic analysis through grounded theory methodology. Not surprisingly, the majority of these books and programs struggle with the inductivist underpinnings of grounded theory. They accept the idea that qualitative researchers should approach their research endeavors with little theoretical preparation, or at least set aside all preconceived notions and build theory from the ground up through brainstorming sessions with small data snippets. The books then offer various methodological heuristics to stimulate theory "discovery."

Adopting methodological steps without a coherent epistemological stance, however, weakens the methodological potential for theory innovation. The problem is not with the specific methodological precepts of coding and memo writing that these methodological intermediaries develop, but with the way the intermediaries are anchored into a more general inductive view of social science, and how such a position then ends up structuring researchers' approach and research design. We thus need to come to terms with the role of induction as a logic of inquiry before we see how methodology operates in a framework of theory construction.

The alternative guidance for theory construction comes from deductive approaches to data analysis. The researcher starts with a strong preexisting theory and aims to modify this theory in light of the research data. The closest manifestation of deductive qualitative research in social science is the extended case method. In spite of its name, this approach is relatively quiet on the nitty-gritty of qualitative research and instead delineates analytical steps to move from observations to broader structural social forces in order to extend one's favorite theory. As we outlined in the introduction, such an approach risks shoehorning ill-fitting data—again affecting the research design that researchers opt for and the theorizations they produce. As with inductive approaches, the problem lies with the logic of inquiry.

This chapter thus takes a critical look at both inductive and deductive approaches to qualitative research, focusing on the ways in which these approaches emerged, on their analytic shortcomings and strengths, and on the way they structure practitioners' research design.

Grounded Theory as Mainstream Qualitative Data Analysis

Barney Glaser and Anselm Strauss's *The Discovery of Grounded Theory* has become not only the gold standard for qualitative data analysis but one of the most cited books in the social sciences.[2] Grounded theory has spread across sociology, nursing and medical research, computer and information sciences, education, law, management, and anthropology. Its coding schemes and heuristic principles have been incorporated into the most widely used qualitative data analysis software programs.[3] Grounded theory has turned into a paradigmatic set of assumptions proclaiming how qualitative analysis should be done; researchers offer an almost obligatory nod to it in the methods section of qualitative research papers whether or not they actually used it.

Historically, grounded theory was located between two competing traditions of mid-century American sociology. Influenced by Paul Lazarsfeld and Robert Merton at Columbia, Glaser emphasized the need for rigorously constructed middle-range theories based on explicit, transparent coding procedures. As a graduate of the University of Chicago's sociology department working with Herbert Blumer and inspired by Robert Park, Strauss stressed the need to capture fundamental social psychological processes as they unfold.[4]

The approach followed Glaser and Strauss's ethnographic study of death and dying in the San Francisco Bay area. In 1958, researchers had declared the sociology of death and dying neglected and barren,[5] but this situation changed in the early 1960s when Glaser and Strauss conducted a study of interactions between dying patients and health care providers in six Bay area hospitals. The study was groundbreaking for substantive and methodological reasons, and their development of "awareness contexts"—patterns of knowledge-relationship among doctors, patients, and families—captured the Zeitgeist by confirming that institutionalized dying led to widespread alienation and isolation. At a time when euphemisms, embellishments, or lies were routinely conveyed to patients about the severity or nature of their diagnosis and prognosis,[6] Glaser and Strauss documented that terminally ill patients often went to great lengths to figure out their status, only to be confronted by a wall of silence from health care providers and complicit family members.[7]

Their analysis, along with Kübler-Ross's[8] influential writings on grief, galvanized a social movement aimed at humanizing dying that took the form of various hospice and palliative care initiatives. Besides crystallizing late modern unease with the medicalization of the dying process, their books[9] aided the emergence of the influential labeling theory, produced a collection of concepts that became part of the sociological canon, and constituted a prime example of the application of a systematic qualitative methodology. Grounded theory, then, was initially intended as a methodological explanation of how the dying studies were conducted, and allegedly reflected Glaser and Strauss's ongoing research experience.[10]

Glaser and Strauss also wrote polemically against what they considered the increasing devaluation of qualitative research. They originally aimed to justify qualitative research against a triple marginalization: theoretical marginalization by functionalist theorists spinning grand theories and looking for straightforward empirical verification; methodological marginalization in which qualitative research was relegated to the production of hypotheses to be tested by statistical quantitative methodologies; and a marginalization within the field of qualitative analysis: ethnographic researchers were said to conduct unsystematic, atheoretical research.

Glaser and Strauss expressed a growing disenchantment with functionalism and survey research.[11] Grounded theory should thus be read alongside other books that came out in the late 1960s: Blumer's manifesto for symbolic interactionism, Peter Berger and Thomas Luckmann's treatise on the social construction of reality, Harold Garfinkel's importation of Schutzian phenomenology into ethnomethodology, and Thomas Kuhn's influential account of scientific revolutions.[12] Unlike these authors, however, Glaser and Strauss offered a realist methodology that aimed to regain qualitative research's legitimacy, ignoring some of the constructivist thrust of the times.

Thus Glaser and Strauss proposed that social scientists build theory "from the ground up" through systematic conceptualization and constant comparisons with similar and distinct research areas. The positivistic tenor is apparent in the privileged position they saw for a disinterested social science researcher and in the emphasis on an inductive methodology uncontaminated by preexisting theories. They advanced a set of methodological principles including theoretical sampling, theoretical saturation, open coding, and memo writing to guarantee that theoretical claims were supported with data. In essence, grounded theory presented an analytical choreography with a deep immersion in data and then a transcendence of this data to reach higher levels of abstraction and generalization. If performed well, the resulting dance emerged from lived experiences, actions, observations, and conversations while researchers simultaneously engaged in conceptually dense and theoretically rich writing.

A keyword search in databases of social science publications suggests that grounded theory did not become the dominant qualitative methodology until the late 1980s, when Strauss published *Qualitative Analysis for Social Scientists*[13] and he and Juliet Corbin issued the user-friendly *Basics of Qualitative Research*.[14] As the titles suggest, both books were foremost methodology books. They pushed the formalization of qualitative methods hinted at in *The Discovery of Grounded Theory* to new levels with research paradigms, analytical matrices, different levels of coding, and systematic memo writing. Key methodological ideas such as theoretical sampling and theoretical saturation also gained prominence. Previously, grounded theory methodological practice had been spread largely through apprenticeship and workshops in San Francisco; these books made it possible for researchers not directly trained by Glaser or Strauss to practice grounded theory. The methods also diffused by way of incorporation in data analysis software programs — especially ATLAS.ti, which was explicitly modeled after a grounded theory analysis, but also other data analysis programs, such as NVivo, Transana, and MAXQDA, which also facilitate and speed up the different steps of coding and memo writing.[15]

In the decades since publication of the original book, the founders of grounded theory have emphasized different epistemological characteristics, and the approach has splintered into a "classic" version associated with Glaser and an "interactionist" variant developed by Strauss and Corbin. The classic version highlights the goal of inductively developing formal theories and revels in the positivist heritage of grounded theory. The key issue, according to Glaser in an acerbic rebuttal to Strauss and Corbin, is to let "categories and their properties emerge which fit and work."[16] The interactionist variant highlights data analysis as interpretative work and pays more attention to the position of the researcher in analyzing data. Kathy Charmaz[17] advanced a "social constructivist" interpretation of grounded theory, and Adele Clarke[18] adapted grounded theory in light of postmodern critiques of qualitative methodology.[19] Among researchers, the variation is even more pronounced. Grounded theory has been used to label any research endeavor that involves coding, any form of qualitative data analysis, and any kind of theory construction. When researchers claim that their work is grounded, it often has little to do with the original methodological precepts; they often use grounded theory simply as a placeholder for methodological legitimacy when writing the methods section.[20]

The Inductive Dilemma of Grounded Theory

Glaser and Strauss perceived a growing division of labor between theorists and empirical researchers in the 1960s when grand theorists such as Talcott Parsons, and Peter Blau created broad "logico-deductive" theories. These theories would then orient the work of empirical researchers in a feedback cycle of verification or refutation. Surveying the theoretical landscape, Glaser and Strauss argued that such an approach led to the development of theories with little connection to substantive social life because researchers would force data into the straightjacket of preexisting concepts.

Instead, they favored generating theories on the basis of the emergence of theoretical categories through a process of constant comparisons between similar observations to develop theoretical properties of an analytic category. *The Discovery of Grounded Theory* contains repeated admonitions not to be led astray by an early commitment to existing theory:

> An effective strategy is, at first, literally to ignore the literature of theory and fact of the area under study, in order to assure that the emergence of categories will not be contaminated by concepts more suited to different areas. Similarities and convergences with the literature can be established after the analytic core of categories has emerged.[21]

Glaser and Strauss posited an "inductive method of theory development" that led through a heuristic process of abstraction to either a substantive or a formal theory:

> To make theoretical sense of so much diversity in his data, the analyst is forced to develop ideas on a level of generality higher in conceptual abstraction than the qualitative material being analyzed. He is forced to bring out underlying uniformities and diversities, and to use more abstract concepts to account for differences in the data.... If the analyst starts with raw data, he will end up initially with a substantive theory.... If he starts with the findings drawn from many studies pertaining to an abstract sociological category, he will end up with a formal theory pertaining to a conceptual area.[22]

They proposed a "constant comparative method" that should be evaluated for transparency of the methodological process and the resulting conceptual framework: "Do the categories fit and work? Are they clearly indicated by data, and do they explain, predict, and interpret anything of significance?"[23] Theoretical sampling suggests sampling comparison groups on the basis of "the *theoretical relevance* for advancing the development of emerging categories."[24] In this way, grounded theory methodologists aspired to produce what Merton called middle-range theories "between highly abstract theory and the multitude of miniscule substantive studies."[25]

At the same time, Glaser and Strauss cryptically noted that theoretical insights require cultivation of a capacity they called "theoretical sensitivity," consisting of the "ability to have theoretical insight into his area of research, combined with an ability to make something of his insights." Theoretical sensitivity expresses itself as an "armamentarium of categories and hypotheses on substantive and formal levels. . . . A discovered, grounded theory, then, will tend to combine mostly concepts and hypotheses that have emerged from the data with some existing ones that are clearly useful." Yet once again, they qualified their call for such theoretical sensitivity with the strong admonition that creativity is lost when social scientists commit themselves to "preconceived," "doctrinaire," or "pet" theories.[26] Thus from the beginning, grounded theory's commitment to an inductive approach created an epistemological and practical dilemma: researchers were admonished to generate new theory without being beholden to preexisting theories, but they still required theoretical sensitivity based on a broad familiarity with existing theories to generate new theories.

This contradictory advice sidestepped a logical problem: induction does not generate theory. Induction helps substantiate generalizations using repeated or accumulated observations: because we have seen several instances of status reversal in interracial marriage, we may presume that status reversal is the norm in interracial marriages. However, inductive logic cannot tell us which objects to focus our attention on, or how we should link the different observations. It doesn't tell us what an "interracial marriage" is, what "status reversal" might be, or how we should go about linking them. Induction, as Peirce put it, is "ampliative"[27]; it strengthens, or "amplifies," our notions of the world by broadening the database. Here, Glaser and Strauss confuse culminating and strengthening substantive theories with the discovery of an entirely new theoretical framework.

Glaser and Strauss's approach to induction resembles that of early empiricist philosophers who contended that the only reliable theories are those generalized from observable data. Francis Bacon argued in his 1620 *Novum Organum* for freeing one's mind from theoretical preconceptions before conducting research, letting go of the "idols" of preconceived notions.[28] However, even at the time, philosophical "rationalists" attacked Bacon's "naïve empiricism," and his philosophy was dealt a devastating blow by Hume's "problem of induction" and Kant's critique of any claim to naturally perceived causal relations.[29] The inductive logic of the tabula rasa could not be sustained. Most social scientists and philosophers of science take as a starting point that observation is necessarily theoretically informed.[30] Induction has an important place in research, but its strength is not in generating new theories.

Most of the primary and secondary literature of grounded theory tried to reconcile the core tension built around induction into the original *Discovery of Grounded Theory*. Various authors suggested a combination of two solutions: embedding basic theoretical frameworks in grounded theory and using heuristic tools to formalize the process of emergence.

As many authors note in this context, early grounded theory was actually not bereft of preconceived theories. The original study on awareness of dying that inspired the grounded theory methodology fits squarely within a second-generation Chicago-school approach that focuses on how the pragmatics of interaction in institutional settings sustain predictable forms of interaction.[31] Glaser and Strauss examined the different perspectives of various actors in the hospital constrained by institutional prerogatives and offered interactional solutions to their predicament—in their case an unequal distribution of information about a terminal condition and the management of timing during the dying process. A similar approach of examining the pragmatics of action and Simmelian interactional forms within institutional settings can be found in the works of their contemporaries.[32]

Subsequent Straussian versions of grounded theory did not necessarily discover new theory but elaborated on a symbolic interactionist theory of action.[33] Several observers argued that grounded theory and symbolic interactionism constitute a yoked theory–methods package.[34] A general focus on interaction, process, meaning of events, and consequences for various actors is grounded in a symbolic interactionist perspective of the world.[35] Recent interpreters of grounded theory have been even more up front about their theoretical allegiances. Charmaz explicitly espouses Blumer's constructivist naturalism in her update of grounded theory, while Clarke presents a pastiche of poststructuralist, postmodernist, actor-network, and symbolic interactionist perspectives in her version of grounded theory.[36] Induction, then, flows from theoretical frameworks that orient the analyst to a general framework of actions, meanings, institutional settings, and silences.

Against this current, Glaser continues to rail against linking grounded theory to a symbolic interactionist or social constructivist perspective.[37] Instead, his solution to the inductivist's dilemma is to offer a generic and formalistic set of coding guidelines, including splitting up coding into theoretical and substantive variants to provide a coding family of causes, context, contingencies, consequences, covariances, and conditions, and to formulate a basic social process[38] that can orient practitioners.[39] This, however, simply pushes the problem one step away. As one observer points out, "a crucial problem with Glaser's list of coding families is that it lacks a differentiation between formal or logical categories and substantial sociological concepts," and thus needs further theoretical elaboration to make the coding schemes work.[40] Others have offered their own heuristic tools. Strauss and Corbin[41] split up coding into open, axial, and selective coding and offered a conditional matrix to help generate inspiration. Working more visually, Clarke suggested situational maps, social world/arenas maps, and positional maps to orient analysis.[42] These authors also offer guidance for memo writing, memo sorting, and diagramming.

Secondary grounded theory literature attempted to bridge the inductive gap between data and analysis with an increasingly more complex and refined set of codes and memos embedded within an implicit, rudimentary theoretical framework. The elaborate coding and memo apparatus has become the hallmark of grounded theory practice and an important reason for its continued popularity and incorporation into leading software programs. More than any other data analytical approach, grounded theory offers a set of seemingly theory-neutral pedagogic and analytical heuristics for qualitative researchers to work with painstakingly gathered materials. These methodological efforts have focused on detailed data analysis but remain sketchy on how they connect to existing theories and facilitate theory construction.

However, is this really a problem? Aren't we taking grounded theory's inductivist brand too seriously? After all, when talking over drinks, grounded theory practitioners readily admit that pure inductivism is impossible and that some theoretical knowledge is necessary. In fact, grounded theory has been taken in so many different directions over the past decade that some of its leading advocates[43] now consider the approach a form of abduction rather than induction, even though Strauss mentioned abduction only once in a limited sense in a footnote[44] and Glaser never broached the topic.

Although shifting the focus to abduction is welcome news, we do not think rebranding the inductivist core of grounded theory solves its epistemological problems. The inductivist legacy infuses research design, the emphasis of data analysis, and the writing up of grounded theory qualitative research. Although practitioners may be told that theoretical sophistication may not be such a bad idea after all, theory gets sidelined after it is mentioned in favor of ever more elaborate coding and memoing practices. This, in turn, reifies the process while sacrificing the very reason grounded theory came into prominence: to explain and encourage theory construction. Although the method was designed as a way to discover theory, such discoveries seem to elude practitioners. The value-oriented logic that may have structured its earliest attempts was gradually replaced by a reification of process. To do justice to the goal of theory construction, we need to deeply rethink the relationship between theory, observation, and methodology.

Can We Solve the Inductive Dilemma with the Extended Case Method?

The inductive program of grounded theory, of course, received it share of criticism. Researchers and theorists from a variety of methodological and epistemological positions pushed against what they saw as its untenable philosophy of science. One of the most important of these critical positions has been a sociological version of a classic anthropological approach, the extended case method.

The extended case method emerged out of the British school of anthropology in the mid-1960s as an alternative to the prevailing structural functionalism of Bronislaw Malinowski and Alfred Radcliffe-Brown and offered a way to study conflicts in communities. In an initial attempt to improve prevailing structural-functional theories, but in reality weakening this paradigm from within, the Manchester school of anthropology introduced the extended case method.[45] Rather than the normative societal order predicted by structural-functional theorists, anthropological fieldworkers had documented repeated instances of conflicts and inconsistencies between norms at their Northern Rhodesia and Nyasaland (now Zambia and Malawi) field sites.

Where many anthropologists were blinded by structural functionalism and ignored or explained away anomalous "disruptive processes," Max Gluckman and Jaap van Velsen, in one of the first moves toward what was later dubbed a poststructuralist anthropology, suggested a different methodological approach to incorporate the study of norm conflicts. Gluckman proposed to empirically study actors through particular incidents and then link the incidents as constitutive of more extended processes in both time and space. Social researchers, they argued, should document a series of disputes, ruptures, and norm conflicts and then record as much of the total context as possible while identifying the main actors. They should be attentive to the ways that individuals exploit norms in ongoing social processes. Theories could then be built from stringing together similar case reports of conflicts over time and space. Van Velsen warned that theoretical approaches should guide but not determine fieldwork.[46] Thus in an exemplary study J. Clyde Mitchell documented witchcraft accusations in a Yao village over an eight-year period.[47] Rather than taking these accusations as isolated instances of sorcery, Mitchell analyzed the charges as a manifestation of fragile village politics, leading over time to the split of the village. He demonstrated that periods of bitter quarrelling are inherent in the life cycle of these villages.

In sociology the major interlocutor of the extended case method has been Michael Burawoy, who encountered some of these anthropologists while conducting fieldwork in former Northern Rhodesia.[48] Whereas Gluckman viewed societal conflicts as expressions of societies, Burawoy saw them as results of external macro forces. Extended case method, according to Burawoy, "applies reflexive science to ethnography in order to extract the general from the unique, to move from the 'micro' to the 'macro,' and to connect the present to the past in anticipation of the future, all by building on preexisting theory."[49] Burawoy's approach consists of four stages in which social researchers move from localized interventions (observations and interviews, called interventions because any attempt to gather data is an intervention in someone's life); to a wider analysis and intervention in regimes of power according to participants' sense of space and time; to broader structuring of external social forces; and finally to reconstructions of existing theory. Burawoy privileges underlying structural conditions in light of the researcher's theory: "*We begin with our favorite theory* but seek not confirmations but refutations that inspire us to deepen that theory. Instead of discovering grounded theory we elaborate existing theory."[50]

The extended case method is mostly compatible with theories that tie observations in the field to larger, usually unobservable patterns of control and macrostructures of domination. Whether in Burawoy's use of Gramsci and neo-Marxist theories of the state and labor, or in the later shift within extended case method toward theories of globalization, the theory answers a question of social ontology—"What does the world look like?" Such neo-Marxist theorization thus provides the denouement of an empirical narrative. It ties ethnographic observations to outside forces. Researchers relying on the extended case method can, in principle, choose among a range of theories, but they must be able to tell in advance what kind of empirical observations *should* be seen in the world. Without this horizon of the what, the research project loses its sharp contours as a problematic empirical case, and theoretical casing becomes impossible.[51]

Extended case method's use of theory is limited if one actually follows Burawoy's four movements of reflexive science, where research moves from an interview or set of observations to an analysis of social processes, then on to social structures, and back into one's theory. It is the third step toward the discovery of underlying structures as modified by broader social forces that requires a theory that privileges macro-structure. This is because, as Burawoy notes, these social forces are often not apparent in the research setting; they "are the effects of other social processes that for the most part lie outside the realm of investigation."[52] Because these social forces may lie outside the consciousness of research populations and the empirical grasp of fieldworkers, they become apparent only through the researcher's adopted theory. The danger, as with the imputations of psychoanalysts, is one of moving from observation to predetermined theorization all too quickly.

In that sense, extended case method is not a solution for the inductive dilemma. Burawoy's rendition of the method limits the creativity of researchers: the researcher approaches the field with a favorite theory, knowing in advance how the field should be extended. The method limits creativity for epistemological reasons, but, as with grounded theory, epistemology spills over into research design. Students of the extended case method are often encouraged to structure their research comparatively, working through what seems to be an interesting variation on a theoretical problem. Doing so tethers researchers to the theoretical framework they began with. After all, a comparison of two or three sites is limited, unless it is strategic for theoretical reasons. A researcher who wishes to change theoretical framing in midresearch will find it virtually impossible to justify the comparison already committed to. The extended case method thus sacrifices the flexibility of qualitative research.

Where Do We Go from Here?

How, then, do theories and methods relate to each other? The grounded theory approach puts its faith in induction. Even when the approach is taken out of an explicit inductive context, the primacy of methodological sequences of coding and memo writing still ascribe conceptual power and innovation to pieces of data that are somehow unencumbered by preexisting theories. The extended case method, in contrast, puts amendment of the researcher's favorite theory at its center. The specific process of theory amendment, however, makes it hard for researchers to develop and change the theoretical framework they began with.

Instead of a choice between induction and deduction, researchers need a logic of inquiry and inference that connects methodology to theory construction. Pragmatist theorizing, with its focus on creativity as a logic of inference, provides us with this leverage. Following Peirce's inferential logic and theory of meaning, methodology becomes critical in eliciting data variation and as a way to allow surprising observations to emerge against a background of existing theorizations. To develop this insight, we first need to revisit the way meaning emerges as the hallmark of qualitative research. Pragmatism offers a distinct take on how meaning making comes about. In the next chapter we explain the rudiments of pragmatist semiotics.

2: SEMIOTICS AND THE RESEARCH ACT

In the last chapter we outlined a plan: we suggested that in order to theorize in qualitative research it is necessary to leave behind both strict inductivism and strict deductivism—both the idea that theory is something that simply mushrooms out of the data, and the notion that we can do research only when we know, more or less, what we expect to find. To arrive at an alternative way to think about the research process, we develop pragmatist philosopher Charles S. Peirce's notion of abduction into abductive analysis, a methodological approach emphasizing a different logic of inference that stands at the basis of theory construction. The road to abduction, however, passes through a much more basic question: How do we construct meaning?[1]

The question of meaning construction is relevant for qualitative data analysis because from the smallest micro-interaction to the most sophisticated global macro-theory, the basic building block of this kind of research is the deciphering and creation of meaning in action. When qualitative researchers conduct interviews, they capture people narrating and interpreting their thoughts and experiences; when researchers observe others, they see people acting out unfolding meaning-making. Moreover, qualitative data analysis is itself a process of meaning-making. In its most generic form, theory construction rests upon the creation of meanings drawn from empirical data in dialogue with an intellectual community. In fact, qualitative research can be thought of as second-order meaning-making: we make meaning of people acting upon meaning during their daily lives. How people construct meaning matters as a foundational unit of analysis and as a core methodological process. In this chapter, we introduce meaning-making as a way to think about the process of theory construction. Chapters 5 and 6 then develop semiotic thinking as a foundational building block for qualitative data analysis.

What Do We Do When We Construct Meaning?

Imagine the following scenario: As you walk down an urban street, you hear someone sitting on the sidewalk saying, "Sir, can you please help me?" As you put your hand in your pocket digging for change, you glance at the person asking you for money. You see a teenage, punk-dressed girl with a pit bull dog, an inordinate number of tattoos, and a cardboard sign with the message "Need $$$. Spaceship ran out of fuel." As you give her a couple of coins, it occurs to you that you have seen quite a few young homeless women with dogs that have an aggressive reputation. You wonder if young homeless women end up keeping aggressive-looking dogs as a way to deter street predators. Also, fleetingly, you wonder whether having a dog is also a way to feel that even though you are down and out and living on the streets, there is a creature that you care for and that cares for you. You remember a homeless man you saw some time ago by the local supermarket, pushing a cart that had a small dog in it.

The memory passes. Soon you begin thinking of the things you are supposed to do at work today, how you will need to respond to an email you ignored yesterday. Then, thinking about your email, you wonder about the funny cardboard sign with its transparent and humorous request for money. You ponder whether these funny requests for money are similar to advertisements, and if they are a way to cement a shared humanity through humor. Then you notice that if you hurry, you might still make the green walk sign at the next intersection, and you walk faster.

What is going on in this situation? This fleeting encounter involved a recalibration of the way you see the world. For a moment, you reflexively took in the situation and tied it to other situations, using a generalization as an explanatory bridge between the cases. In a mundane, everyday way, this everyday incident moved you toward the construction of theory. You isolated an occurrence from the stream of experiences that you encounter in the world, treated it as data and then explicitly generalized it to form tentative ideas about the world.

Although there are important differences between the disciplined acts of theory construction in social science work and everyday perceptions and generalizations, this episode tells us something important about the craft of theorizing and about the relationship between data and theory. Qualitative research aims to come to terms with observations. In conducting and analyzing research, we often try to convince ourselves, and later our readers, that these empirical observations tell us something beyond the particular instances that we have been privy to. Much as we do in our everyday life, we assume that the things we see, hear, and otherwise experience signify something. Our observations are indicative of a larger pattern. Theory construction, in these terms, is the production of an understanding, of a new claim regarding the empirical world, that we hope others will take up, argue with, refute, or employ.

Although Peirce's semiotics evolved over his lifetime and included many false starts and multiple subdivisions that befuddle even the best of Peirce scholars, his basic insights remained both clear and striking. As a way to ground the logic of scientific inquiry, Peirce broke down different aspects of meaning-making-in-action. As opposed to the later division of the sign into the signified and the signifier, associated with the work of Ferdinand de Saussure,[2] Peirce devised a threefold partition. He wrote:

> I define a sign as anything which is so determined by something else, called its Object, and so determines an effect upon a person, which effect I call its interpretant, that the latter is thereby mediately determined by the former.[3]

Meaning-making thus consists of three interlinked parts: a sign, an object, and an interpretant. The first of these elements is the sign, which we can think of as the signifier in the same way that smoke signifies a fire or that a word signifies a concept or object. The sign does not exist on its own but is always in relationship to an object. It is the utterance, the pointing finger, the picture, or whatever vehicle represents an object in a certain way. The second related element is then the object, any entity about which a sign signifies. The object is taken very broadly; it can be an actual thing "out there," an individual, a word, or an idea in our head.

Peirce's key insight, however, was that meaning-making is not an abstract but a practical achievement, occurring in action. To capture this aspect Peirce argued that every act of meaning-making needs an interpretant—the effect of the sign-object through which meaning-making receives its definition. The interpretant is a transformation that the interpreter undergoes while making sense of a sign. Simply put, a sign is not a part of an act of signification unless it has some kind of effect—an understanding, emotion, or action.[4] The interpretant does not have to be a cognitive interpretation of the sign-object, although it can be, and often is, an understanding. Instead, it is the way the sign-object effects a change in the world, whether as the most complex act of textual interpretation or as the simplest and most unreflexive gesture.[5]

Peirce semiotics is thus fundamentally triadic: a sign stands *for* something *to* something. If you eliminate the object or the interpretant, there is no longer a signification process (see figure 1).[6] In our example of the young

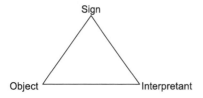

FIGURE 1. Peirce's semiotic triad. The sign, the object, and the interpretant are intrinsically connected.

woman begging for spare change, the object consists of the entire material tableau of girls with tattoos and dogs. The signs are the question "Sir, can you please help me?" reinforced with the handwritten cardboard note, both of which focus our attention on a particular aspect of the situation. The interpretant is our immediate translation of the object-sign into a request for money, our habitual digging in our pockets for change, as well as our half-baked ruminations about the presence of dogs as protection and as animals to care for. Meaning-making depends on the intertwining of the three components taken together.

Peirce then made a second crucial move in his semiotics: the interpretant can always become the sign for another iteration of meaning-making. To understand this, think about a conversation: it is usually structured by people elaborating upon others', as well as their own, past utterances. Each utterance is taken as the grounds for the next, closing some possible interpretations and opening others. Any sustained thought, indeed every daydream, proceeds in that way, moving from image to image, or from one syllogism to the next. In the spare-change example, we came to think about advertisements via remembering emails that we had to write and the funny phrase on the cardboard sign. Meanings are thus strung together in semiotic chains, and temporal movement is intrinsic to meaning-making.

The interpretant does not have to become a new sign, however. Conversations may dead-end, and actions based on signs may fail to lead to a new signifying moment. Again, the scenario above is instructive: which one thought led to the next—one interpretant bringing up memories and acting as a sign for the next interpretant—the spiral of meaning-making was cut short. After a few seconds spent elaborating the meaning of the begging situation, we find ourselves distracted by the world or by our own ongoing projects. The practicalities of traffic and our work responsibilities interrupted our stream of thinking. Meaning-making is then an open and ongoing process rather than an action in which we define a single correct designation of meaning. In short, the interpretant is foremost an effect that completes meaning-making. It refers to an act, whether visible or invisible, evoked by the sign-object. Peirce thus theorizes a highly contingent and interactional schema of the process of meaning-making.[7]

The constitutive elements and relations of meaning-making offer a vantage point to marshal semiotics for theory construction. The general contours of meaning-making in everyday life carry over to interpretation in qualitative data analysis. As other theorists have already noted,[8] there is no sharp break between what we do as social scientists and what we do when we take off our professional cap. Interpretation in qualitative data analysis is a purposeful, systematic, and disciplined form of meaning-making predicated on the same processes as those of everyday meaning-making. Qualitative researchers notice and record observations and construct a semiotic chain that may lead to new and generalized interpretants.

In order to get a stronger semiotic purchase on the act of theorizing, we move to a finer level of resolution, looking at the interpretant and the relationship in the triad more closely.[9] This allows us to bring out a more specific dimension in meaning-making, transitioning from the initial potential of meaning-making to the actual encounter with the sign-object, and leading up to a theoretical generalization.[10] This dynamic movement from potentiality to actualization and generalization highlights a key tension both in everyday meaning-making and in qualitative data analysis, a tension between our ability to imbue the world with meaning and the world's resistance to such attempts. Qualitative data analysis requires freedom to produce interpretants of what a data object may signify but requires also sensitivity to constraints inherent to the actual observed encounters. The trick is to stimulate creativity without letting one's imagination run wild.

The Sign-Object Relationship

As a way to start unpacking how Peirce's theory of meaning-making further informs the theorization of qualitative research, let us start with the relationship between object and sign. An object—either an abstract idea or a physical thing—is not only "filled" with meaning by the sign. True, when we signify an object, we point toward a specific aspect of it. And yet, the object must be understood as an active part of the puzzle of meaning-making. Even as we signify it, the properties of the object put some constraints on the signs.[11] Even the most whimsical, unexpected, aberrant sign is somewhat limited by the properties of the object. Objects, moreover, act back and defy our expectations and signification. Meaning-making occurs partly in the tension between how the object is represented by the sign and the resistance it offers action. The panhandling woman with an aggressive dog who is sitting on a street corner asking for spare change is not endlessly interpretable, especially not in the specific ethnographic moment of accosting a passerby.

Of course, any object can be signified in numerous, if not infinite, ways—

and can evoke multiple interpretants. The panhandling woman's dog may provoke my thoughts about protection or care; it may be seen as a vector of potential neglect for a passing animal rights advocate; or it may be a source of danger to a dad walking his toddler around the block. And it may signify all of these interpretants at the exact same time. Still, the animal's characteristics as a dog, the fact that it seemed to cuddle up to the girl, and the choker chain around its neck all shape the range of possible signs. The object thus poses certain parameters on each sign for it to be able to represent this particular object for an interpretant. If I point at something, the interpretant is shaped not only by what I happen to point at, but by the perceptual affordances[12] that the object itself provides. In symbolic communication, flexibility and polysemy of meaning may seem to be the rule, and a wide margin of interpretation to be the order of the day. Talk, however, is also predictably restrained by dominant understandings and the practical consequences for action they entail.

Moreover, since we are enmeshed in a social world, the interpretant is also constrained by the consequences we anticipate our actions will have. Think of the following two examples. First, in his study of an American town in the 1980s, Theodore Caplow[13] showed that even though residents of "Middletown" often said that they didn't care much for Christmas gifts, when Christmastime came, they still bought gifts as much as everybody else did. The reason for this was clear: although some residents thought Christmas gifts were overrated, they expected their parents-in-law to value these gifts and to treat their failure to buy gifts as indicative of disregard or disrespect. When they weighted lofty ideals against angry in-laws, the preferred course of action became all too clear.

A similar process can be seen in one of the authors' projects, analyzing condom use in sub-Saharan Africa.[14] Although people in Malawi increasingly say that condoms should be used even in potentially committed relationships, when the time came to consummate a relationship, partners expected that if they insisted on condom use, their partner would think either that they are infected or that they are just in it for a one-night stand. In both cases, an object—condom use or Christmas gifting practices—resists people's attempts to signify it in a specific way. Objects resist materially but are also already enmeshed in a world of meaning. Such expectations about expectations powerfully channel action into culturally recognizable forms that may have little to do with how either condoms or gifting is potentially perceived.

How do these considerations relate to the research act? The key issue is the obduracy of the object in relation to how researchers would have wanted it to be understood by the sign. Meaning-making in qualitative research is partly about open-ended brainstorming about the potential meanings of a piece of data. Theory can be used to resignify the world around us; it helps to abstract and describe objects.[15] The resistance that empirical evidence offers limits and recursively shapes the resignification of the object. The upshot of the sign-object relationship for data analysis is that it takes advantage of the resistance that objects offer to interpretations. There are always multiple ways to understand an observation, a snippet of action, and an interaction. However, to say that there are multiple ways to signify an observation is *not* to say that either our intended interpretations or those of actors in the field will prevail. Like the actors we follow in the field or through the archives, we are constrained by the affordances of objects. Not everything goes. The object in qualitative research limits the interpretations we can project. Methods can be seen as a way to codify and offer trials of strength to increase the precision of our understanding of the object. If our acts of signification pass such methodological trials, we will have a better sense of what kinds of plausible theoretical narratives fit the phenomena we are examining.[16]

The emphasis on the resistance of the object, however, may raise a problem, which we may call, following philosopher Wilfrid Sellars,[17] "the myth of the given." If the object is all there is to the production of knowledge, we are assuming not only a simple realist world—one in which patterns and relations exist out there irrespective of the analyst—but also a positivist one, a world in which we can come to know the real objects and relations out there by using the tools of science. Both these positions, as we outlined in the last chapter, are best avoided. The way in which Peirce's semiosis avoids a naive version of realism, and rejects positivism point blank, is in the introduction of the interpretant and its relation to habits of thought and action.[18]

Interpretants, Semiotic Chains, and Habits of Thought and Action

If the object provides us with a way to think of the resistance that forces our hand, the interpretant allows us to appreciate the creativity inherent in meaning-making. The interpretant, as we outlined above, is the effect of the sign-object: the understanding, emotion, or action that emerges when the sign-object is taken up in the world. And as in the relation between sign and object, the sign-object also shapes and constrains the range of possible interpretants. Yet our actions are not completely defined by the sign or by the resistance of the object. If interpretation and action were direct consequences of the sign-object, we would be living in a crude behaviorist world devoid of much creativity. And yet the way we act upon the sign-object is often quite surprising. It is precisely because of the interplay among sign, object, and interpretant—as these are affected by actors' habits of thought and action—that novel theorizations are possible.

Interpretants come in many shapes. We already noted that they may be a feeling, an action, a train of thought. They can also differ in the degree to which they are relevant or consequential for future action. We can capture this variety with the opening scenario involving the woman asking for spare change. In reacting, you made a series of calibrations of your view of the world. In a way similar to the act of theorization in qualitative research, the interpretant emerged as a budding generalization. Rather than being only a habitual or emotional reaction, the interpretant involved an evaluation of a world in which young women, homelessness, dogs, violence, cardboard signs, and emotional ties intersected in a novel way. But we can imagine that someone who is inured by the many beggars in U.S. cities and who is expecting a panhandler at this particular spot might simply reach into her purse or pocket and toss some coins without giving it any more thought. In this case, there is surely an embodied perception and action, but it does not change the person's relation to the world in any conscious way. If interrupted and asked why she gave change to the woman, the passerby could have reflected on her habit of giving money to panhandlers, and may have constructed a viable vocabulary of motive,[19] but if she was not asked, the event might never have surfaced into reflection. It happened, and was done with.

The shape the interpretant ends up taking is thus defined partly by the sign-object, but is also replete with the entire history of action, interpretation, and inference that interpreters bring to the observation—their habits of thought and action and the surprising possibilities these afford. Every interpretant that emerges in the process of human communication refracts the sign-object through the lens of the interpreter's particular proto-theoretical categories, preconceived notions, habits, and preferences. The interpreter perceives and acts in ways that are culturally shared and ready to hand—as Christmas gifts are associated with family relations in some circles and condoms with one-night stands in others. These encodings may even attain a taken-for-granted character to the point that they seem to have become one with the object. The interpretant is also dependent on personal, cultivated ways of perceiving: through personal histories, theoretical proclivities, even moods.[20]

In spite of the constraints objects put on signs and signs on interpretants, the creativity of meaning-making requires the full set of biographical, cognitive, and affective issues the interpreter brings to semiosis. Signification is not an isolated act but part of an ongoing flow of action in which signs build on each other. Our emphasis on the interpretant in qualitative research

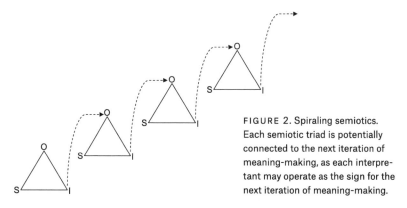

FIGURE 2. Spiraling semiotics. Each semiotic triad is potentially connected to the next iteration of meaning-making, as each interpretant may operate as the sign for the next iteration of meaning-making.

highlights the complementary relationship between observation and inference—specifically, the critical role of the act of observing.

A useful way to conceptualize the relation between our inferences is to draw out the semiotic chains these produce. Peircean semiotics can be imagined as a spiral of meaning-making where the interpretant of one iteration of meaning-making may potentially become the sign for another, as illustrated in figure 2. However, this spiraling view of meaning-making doesn't tell us what we are spiraling toward. What is the direction of the spiral? What accounts for the endless permutations of meaning-in-action that our lives are made of? The sign-object obviously affects the direction of meaning-making in the grounds of the object presented by the sign. The fact that the homeless woman's dog was sitting by her side, and the words on the sign she carried obviously shaped the way we saw her and our subsequent ruminations about her life. This, in itself, is not enough. We may spiral to heights of theoretical sophistication or into intellectual oblivion. Simply having a dog and a sign does not completely define our reaction to the woman, the dog, or the sign.

What Peirce's designation of the interpretant allows us to think about is precisely the ways in which characteristics of the interpreter and the sign refract the object in action. The direction of the spiraling of meaning-making—the actual consequences-in-action that make the world around us meaningful—is thus an outcome of the directions of the object and the history, embodied knowledge, and habits of thought and action of the person acting upon this sign-object.

Think of the sign as one determinant of the vector of meaning-making, presenting the basic grounds for understanding the object. In the panhandling example, the sign "Need $$$. Spaceship ran out of fuel" alerts us to some aspects of the situation (our shared humanity, for instance). Then again, the object is another such determinant that may change the potential direction of meaning-making through its resistance. In this case, for example, the dog sitting beside the sign may not have been part of the intended message but still caught our attention. These elements are insufficient to predict the effect they will provoke in passersby. The interpretant is finally produced by the interrelation among the sign, the object, and the characteristics of the interpreter (the interpreter's habits of thought and action), some of which may be cultivated within the interaction itself. Different interpretants allow meaning-making to spiral in different directions, and this—far from being a weakness—is precisely what allows for both creativity and good social science.

Understanding meaning-making as a semiotic chain provides a way to think about how novel interpretations emerge. Theorizing in qualitative research amounts to a disciplined way to use observations and encase them in multiple ways, to present multiple vectors of meaning-making from various perspectives while checking them against the resistance of observations in the field. Thus when researchers work with data, they test and retest different ways to construct chains of meaning.

Creative inference—the construction of new theoretical insights—is predicated on this relation among sign, object, and interpretant.[21] The goal of a theoretically infused logic of research is to make this relation as productive as possible. Although the impetus for creativity cannot be completely codified, there are ways to organize qualitative research to make this semiotic interplay generative. As we return to the same observation, artificially construct notes and memos, think through different theoretical insights, carefully look at variation among observations, and encounter skepticism and advice from our peers, we provide a research environment that allows us to think and rethink the objects of our research. In the end, these methodological precepts allow us to act on our observations in ways that make them cases of different theoretical accounts and, finally, that allow us to provide a compelling theoretical generalization from our data.

Making Use of Peirce's Semiotics in the Field

In order to breathe life into Peirce's concepts, we show how they can be used to help unravel the ways actors in the field give meaning to striking encounters with others. We use one of the classic articles in the sociology of deviance—Fred Davis's "Deviance Disavowal"[22]—to draw attention to the central tension between the obduracy of sign-objects and the creative appropriation of signs. Davis offers an everyday example that shows how people in a semiotically overdetermined predicament are occasionally able to resignify their situation. Although Davis references later pragmatists such as G. H. Mead and his followers, we show that the use of Peirce's categories renders the analysis precise and insightful.

Davis was interested in how people with visible impairments—people who were blind, in a wheelchair, or otherwise visibly disabled—managed interactions with nondisabled people whom they didn't know well. As Davis soon realized, the recurring problem facing these men and women was that in almost every situation in which they interacted with someone they didn't already know, their disability instantly became the focus of attention. The disability, as Davis put it, "inundated" the interaction. The nondisabled people often started talking about the disability, whether or not the people with a disability wanted to talk about it. Or, even worse, they pretended to ignore the disability while acting in ways that made it obvious that they were acutely aware of it.

The practical problem of how to behave around people with disabilities extended beyond how others perceived the person with a disability. With the heavy cultural baggage that being "crippled" carried, the nondisabled "normals" were trapped in an interaction in which they didn't know how to act. The result was "a pronounced stickiness of interactional flow and the embarrassment of the normal by which he conveys the all too obvious message that he is having difficulty in relating to the handicapped person."[23] Of course, the interactional problem was more acute for the people with disabilities than for the nondisabled: after all, the nondisabled found themselves only rarely in this uncomfortable sort of interaction, and it was not their identity that was on the line. The visibly disabled, however, were tired of being perceived primarily as "handicapped people." Thus, for example, a man using a wheelchair told of people who pretended not to notice his disability:

> I get suspicious when somebody says, "Let's go for a uh, ah [imitates confused and halting speech] push with me down the hall," or something like that. This to me is suspicious because it means that they're aware, really aware, that there's a wheelchair here, and that this is probably uppermost with them. . . . A lot of people, in trying to show you that they don't care that you're in a chair, will do crazy things. Oh, there's one person I know who constantly kicks my chair, as if to say "I don't care that you're in a wheelchair. I don't even know that it's there." But that is just an indication that he really knows it's there.[24]

Other interviewees narrated that regardless of what else they may be, others first and foremost see them as handicapped:

One informant, a strikingly attractive girl, reports that she frequently elicits from new acquaintances the comment, "How strange that someone so pretty should be in a wheelchair." Another informant, a professional worker for a government agency, tells of the fashionable female client who after having inquired on how long the informant had been in her job remarked, "How nice that you have something to do."[25]

From a semiotic perspective, the challenge people with disabilities faced is that of the disability's culturally encoded resistance to their attempt to signify the situation differently. Whatever self they wished to present or whatever sign they constructed, their disability was what primarily defined the interpretant. And as the interpretant became the sign for the next iteration of meaning-making, the disability came to dominate the interaction for both parties in the interaction.

Thus in the first excerpt, none of the interlocutors explicitly talked about the wheelchair, but the actions of the nondisabled still turned the disability into the most salient aspect of the interaction. No matter what this man said, no matter what signs he produced, his interlocutor's interpretant was defined by an image of him as wheelchair-bound. As the second excerpt then shows, when a different aspect of selfhood emerges—the girl's good looks, or a career job, for example—it is immediately juxtaposed with the disability, leading to an inescapable semiotic dilemma.

Following his interviewees' lead, Davis moves next to the question of normalization, or to use his term, "deviance disavowal." Given that these semi-anonymous encounters are both common and frustrating, how do people with disabilities manage their interactions to make their disability no longer the focal point? Is it possible to subvert or reorient the semiotic cycle? How can a person take charge of the way sign-objects are taken up?

The visibly disabled people Davis interviewed tried to normalize interaction in myriad ways. As in most semiotic operations, there is a vast array of possible approaches to a situation, which will meet with varying levels of success. Two issues stand out in Davis's description of these semiotic strategies. First, in most cases normalization is a multistage process. People with disabilities would begin by relying on the "fictional acceptance" that nondisabled interlocutors feigned, using it as an opening to subvert the semiotic cycle. Although they did not buy into fictional acceptance or treat it as actual acceptance, they used the fiction to construct new signs. Second, the people with disabilities tried to reframe their interactions so the disability wasn't the only thing their interlocutors attended to. They tried to tap into other aspects of their interlocutors' habits of thought and action to create a commonality with them.

One way people with disabilities would try to take control over such an interaction was to raise the issue of the disability explicitly but humorously. Davis writes that one respondent who used a wheelchair often called his interlocutors "'good-leggers,' an in-group term from his rehabilitation hospital days, which along with 'dirty normals' he sometimes uses with new acquaintances 'because it has a humorous connotation . . . and lots of times it puts people at their ease.'"[26] By using humor, this interviewee and others exposed their disabilities interactionally. Paradoxically, it is precisely by outing their disabilities that they become able to transcend them in interaction. The man with the wheelchair was "letting the normal know that he does not take offense at the latter's uneasiness or regard it as a fixed obstacle toward achieving rapport."[27] Even more to the point, in these situations the people with disabilities constructed a commonality: by laughing at the disabling condition together with their interlocutors, they instantly created a self that shared something with them, precisely the problem they were trying to solve.

Other normalization techniques include trying to appear cool even when placed in an uncomfortable situation, or trying to hang out with someone who is obviously nonstigmatized and normalizing interaction through association. In all of these,

> The fashioning of shared perspectives also implies a progressively more binding legitimation of the altered self-representations enacted in the encounter; that is, having once normalized his perception of the handicapped person, it becomes increasingly more compromising—self-discrediting, as it were—for the normal to revert to treating him as a deviant again.[28]

In other words, once the vector of the semiotic chain had been altered, it is increasingly difficult for the nondisabled person to explicitly reorient to the disability; the weight of interactional embarrassment has effectively shifted.

Our reinterpretation of Davis's work exemplifies both the constraints and the creative possibilities of semiotic categories to shape and influence everyday interactions. People with visible disabilities are often stuck in situations where their disabled status inundates interaction. And yet an opening for a semiotic transformation arises from the fact that out of courtesy or unease nondisabled interactants pretend to ignore the disabilities. People with disabilities can turn such fictional acceptance into more explicit acceptance of themselves as multifaceted people by calling upon other cultural associations or by subverting the ongoing semiotic chain of meaning-making. Davis' research then demonstrates the central dynamic of meaning-making as a way not only to produce predictability but also to introduce some unexpectedness in everyday life. As people with disabilities succeed in converting such situations, their interlocutors will see them and their world differently, if only briefly.

Revealing the semiotic dimensions and ironies of encounters between visibly disabled and nondisabled people has been politically influential. To contemporary readers Davis's analysis may take disability as a biological category for granted, and his association of disability with deviance may seem wrong, but this more than fifty-year-old article helped crystallize a social movement of people with disabilities by focusing on the extensive work people with disabilities routinely do to put others at ease. Davis's and later Goffman's work on stigma paved the way for the "social model of disability," which forcefully articulated that disability resides largely in the inability of the social environment to accommodate certain differences in interaction. Although physical, intellectual, psychological or other variations may lead to limitations, these do not necessarily need to be disabilities in an inclusive society. This social model stands in opposition to a medical model that locates disability mainly in bodily functional impairments. Here social science analysis offered a counter frame of disability that suggested disability policies centered on institutional accommodation and modification.

Like the disabled actors' operations of meaning, social scientists' acts of meaning-making—including the questions of which theory to use, how to look at observations, and how and whether to change theoretical standpoints during the research process—are semiotic operations. Yet there are predictable variations on the semiotic theme. In contrast to the interactions that the people with disabilities recounted, Davis fixed the interaction between himself and the interviewees by recording and transcribing interviews. His theoretical conclusions are carefully substantiated with interview excerpts—which serve as synecdoche for the data he had in his files. And then there are more hidden differences that the final product only hints at: a footnote in which he thanks Sheldon Messinger for an insight, references to a not-yet-published paper by Goffman, and the incorporation of peer-reviewer comments and criticisms that authors invariably receive. These barely acknowledged differences suggest more fundamental divergences between everyday and social science meaning-making processes that influenced Davis as an interpreter of social science observations. In the next chapter, we show how a pragmatist standpoint theorizes a logic of inquiry that facilitates the construction of new and generalized forms of inference in action.

3: ABDUCTION AND MULTIPLE THEORIES

In order to incorporate a pragmatist perspective into a qualitative research program aimed at theory construction, we need to make the inferential logic at the basis of research explicit. To do so, we highlight what Peirce called *abduction*, the inferential procedure through which people in their everyday life as well as social-scientists-at-work produce novel generalizations about the world they live in. These generalizations are necessarily embedded in theorizations of the world, whether in the form of embodied hunches or in the shape of full-blown theories. We produce theoretically inspired accounts of the social world, whether we want to or not.

Some of the most important differences between everyday generalizations and what we do as qualitative researchers lie in the way we use theory. Do we explicitly aim to construct theoretical generalizations or provisionally solve practical puzzles? Do we systematically gather observations? Do we deliberately prepare to stimulate moments of insight? How do such insights then recursively affect our research design? Developing this aspect of the logic of inquiry allows us to clarify what we mean by theory to stimulate abductive insights, and why we argue that in order to do justice to the process of research, social scientists need to move from a singular theory to multiple theoretical perspectives.

The Logic of Abduction

Thinking about the place of theory in the research process has long been held hostage by a distinction between coming up with novel theories and the process of turning these theories into defensible scientific findings. Of the two operations, only the second was considered the proper domain of science and the philosophy of science. As Karl Popper, one of the most important philosophers of science in the twentieth century, put it, "The initial stage, the act of conceiving or inventing a theory, seems to me neither to call for logical analysis nor to be susceptible of it."[1] In order to delineate the realm of science, Popper and others thus sharply separated an initial "context of discovery"—a messy realm of intuitions, flashes of insight, and other nonlogical operations—from "the context of justification," the proper realm of the philosophy of science.

In this view, science starts where discovery ends:

> Discovery concerns the origin, creation, genesis, and invention of scientific theories and hypotheses. Justification concerns their evaluation, test, defense, success, truth, and confirmation. Discovery is for description alone, for psychology and the history of the sociology of science. Justification, however, is for the philosophy of science and epistemology.[2]

For Popper and others, the realm of science was limited to the process of deductively testing hypotheses in order to see whether they could be falsified through what he termed "critical tests"—tests that would potentially be able to refute a theory. They thus paid little attention to where hypotheses came from. The key was that once a hypothesis was formulated, and only then, it required systematic testing to see whether it could be falsified. If it was falsified by a critical test we should go back to our drawing boards; if it wasn't, we could hold it as true until further notice. This Popperian image of science is a clean one. It isn't, however, very helpful if we want to understand theorizing. It also happens not to be a very good approximation of the actual work of scientists as they theorize and empirically investigate their findings.[3]

In contrast to such a division of labor between discovery and justification, Peirce treated scientific work as an ongoing act in which discovery and justification are inseparable and intertwined moments. Instead of ignoring discovery or relegating it to the sidelines of the serious business at hand, Peirce pointed out a logic of the creative aspects of scientific discovery and constructed a unified context of research within which discovery and justification intersect. His approach rested upon abduction, or a "leading away," according to the term's Latin etymology (which explains why it is used for both inference and aliens). As Peirce put it, abduction denotes the "process of forming an explanatory hypothesis"[4] when confronted with a set of unexplainable observations. According to Peirce's formulation, abduction is the only logical mechanism that introduces new ideas into a scientific body of knowledge.[5]

Abduction has a logical form distinct from both induction and deduction. Deductive reasoning begins with a rule, proceeds through a case, then arrives at an observed result that either demonstrates the plausibility of the rule or falsifies it. Thus, the general form of deduction is as follows:

All A are B (all people are mortal).
C is A (Socrates is a person).
Thus, C is B (Socrates is mortal).

Induction, in contrast, starts with a collection of given cases and proceeds with examination of their implied results, to allow the inference that some universal rule is operative:

All observed A are C (all observed swans are white).
Thus, all A are C (all swans are white).

The inductive rule gains plausibility with the multiplication of cases, although induction cannot explain the definition of A and C or the connection between the two. Thus, in the example above, to define what a swan is may seem straightforward, yet it requires a typology of birds. We have to assume, at the very least, that color does not define the bird as a swan; otherwise our claim would be tautological. We would also need a typology of the species that denies entry to, for example, a duck or a crow.

Lastly, Peirce observed, the logical operation he termed abduction starts with consequences and then constructs reasons:

The surprising fact C is observed.
But if A were true, C would be a matter of course.
Hence, there is a reason to suspect that A is true.[6]

In other words, abduction is the form of reasoning through which we perceive an observation as related to other observations, either in the sense that there is an unknown cause and effect hidden from view or in the sense that the phenomenon is similar to other phenomena already experienced and explained.[7] Importantly, as opposed to both induction and deduction, the proposition A is neither assumed before the fact (as it is in deduction) nor observed (as it ideally is in induction). Rather, the proposition is guessed at, presumed after the fact to explain observations we cannot easily explain away. Peirce explained how abduction works in scientific research:

A mass of facts is before us. We go through them. We examine them. We find them a confused snarl, an impenetrable jungle. We are unable to hold them in our minds. We endeavor to set them down upon paper; but they seem so multiplex intricate that we can neither satisfy ourselves that what we have set down represents the facts, nor can we get any clear idea of what it is that we have set down. But suddenly, while we are poring over our digest of the facts and are endeavoring to set them into order, it occurs to us that if we were to assume something to be true that we do not know to be true, these facts would arrange themselves luminously. That is abduction.[8]

The question of how innovative A is, or where exactly it comes from, remains an issue of debate. We can read Peirce's syllogism of abduction as presuming that we are already familiar with potential explanations for anomalous findings. Abduction is then simply the extension of an existing theory to a new substantive area when we encounter a surprising observation. As William James beautifully put it, "Our minds thus grow in spots; and like grease-spots, the spots spread."[9] Others, and this is the interpretation we will build upon here, emphasize that although our habits obviously play a role in theorizing, abduction captures the process of coming up with A, including the process in which a truly novel theory is created, which leaves room for innovation. Either way, the abductive proposition A is a sufficient but not a necessary account for the existence of C. There may always be other abductions, other ways to explain and encase "the confused snarl" of observations before us.

In his later writings, Peirce considered abduction the first step in a methodological process of scientific inquiry that also required induction and deduction. Once a hypothesis has been formed abductively, deduction helps work out the hypothesis by providing a plausible set of predictions about what should happen (or what should have happened). Induction then constitutes the evaluation of these hypotheses as it provides the data that should conform to the deductively delineated premise. Abduction is the most conjectural and weakest of the three modes of inference because it seeks a situational fit between observed facts and general rules without recourse to the explanatory proposition to begin with. Abduction, Peirce noted, provided less certainty than induction, and both are less secure than deduction, but abduction is the only inferential operation that has any innovative potential. Induction is able to classify only by grouping particulars in a deductively preformed general category, while abduction formulates the explanation, the category into which observations will fall. Abduction suggests explanations, which are then formalized into deductions, while induction confirms them through empirical testing: "Abduction seeks a theory. Induction seeks for facts."[10]

It becomes clear, when this point of view is adopted, that people constantly perform abduction in their everyday lives, continuously recalibrating their expectations of the world when they face surprising phenomena. You put a child to bed, hear a loud boink noise followed by hysterical crying, and presume that the child fell out of bed. Or you look outside in the morning and note that the lawn is wet and infer that it rained during the night. In both cases other abductions are possible—a bookcase in your child's room might have fallen, scaring your child; your next-door neighbor may have decided to water your lawn out of frustration with your wilting patches of what should have been lush grass. Abduction is everywhere, in any case where we introduce an interpretant that wasn't already explicitly produced by the sign-object in order to tell a narrative or to produce an abstraction or generalization about the world.

Peirce conceptualized the process of abduction as both a logical inference and a flash of insight:

> It is an act of *insight*, although of extremely fallible insight. It is true that the different elements of the hypothesis were in our minds before; but it is the idea of putting together what we had never before dreamed of putting together which flashes the new suggestion before our contemplation.[11]

The problem is not so much to come up with a good hypothesis but to decide which hypothesis is worth pursuing.[12] How do we decide on a particular abductive inference, and why it is that from a universe of endless possible directions, our abductions often seem uncannily precise?

The Origins of Abductive Insights

Even Peirce's most avid supporters consider his answer to the question of how to come up with a hypothesis the most problematic part of his philosophical writings on abduction.[13] Because "trillions of trillions of hypotheses"[14] are always possible, Peirce reverted to a unity of human and nature justified through his understanding of evolutionary thinking. As we are already within nature, we have acquired through the process of evolution an "affinity" to the way things actually work around us. "Man has a certain Insight, not strong enough to be oftener right than wrong, but strong enough not to be overwhelmingly more often wrong than right."[15] Much like William James, Peirce assumed that the complexity of the human mind implies a proliferation of instincts. He saw an "innate tendency toward a positive truth"[16] as such an instinct. After all, as he put it, if chickens know from birth the "correct" grains to peck, "why should you think that to man alone this gift is denied?"[17]

Peirce's writings on abduction thus provide a direction for thinking about the logic of theoretical innovation and for tying together the context of discovery and the context of justification. But his shaky assumptions regarding the source of abductive reasoning result in an epistemological dead end.[18]

If we posit a natural instinct for truth through which new ideas come into being, we introduce a term rather than solve a problem. Instead of using Peirce's pragmatism to clarify qualitative research, abductive reasoning would become only a mystical assurance that new ideas are available, waiting to be instinctually plucked from the tree of knowledge. To make abduction pragmatically generative, the source of the abductive process should be reformulated, bracketing any natural affinity between person and world.

The biological-instinctual form of reasoning, however, was not the sole one Peirce used. He also acknowledged a much more plausible and deeply social form of reasoning. Thus in some writings Peirce stated that instincts should not be considered only as biological tendencies people are born with, but should also include the tendencies and habits of action that people develop throughout their lives. Thus, the "rational instinct" is not a given, and any innate "tendency toward a positive truth" is achieved through a cultivated perceptual insight, so that "abductive inference shades into perceptual judgments."[19]

This view of the origins of abduction is in line with William James's core idea that habits of thought are the key to understanding theoretical innovation. Following this lead, abduction should be understood as a continuous process of forming conjectures about a world; conjectures that are shaped by the solutions a researcher already has or can make ready to hand—immediately available as a schema of perception and action.[20] Thus, we argue that the precondition for abductive reasoning is not natural instinct but socially cultivated and cultivatable ways of seeing. When socially produced knowledge is substituted for instinct, abduction is based on socially located, positional knowledge that can be deepened and marshaled for the purpose of theory construction. The interpretant, in this case, is constructed through the interplay of empirical observations and the experiences, ways of perceiving, and habits of thought that the social scientist cultivates over time.

These aspects of abductive reasoning bring us to the literature on positionality in sociology and anthropology, where much is made of the fact that the researcher is part of the world of the people she studies. This being-in-the-world is far from being a guarantor for truth in any transcendent sense. Rather, it is a core issue to be grappled with, inevitably leading to partial and historically situated insights, and provoking questions of scientific authority and representation. Thinking through the question of positionality, the literature on qualitative research has called for diverse forms of epistemological accountability, where critically interrogating a researcher's biography, sympathies, intentions, and procedural principles offers a clarification of the position from which knowledge had been culled.[21]

Although often masked by complex jargon and internal academic rivalries, the arguments forwarded within the literature on positionality are straightforward. These approaches first note that we always occupy a certain set of social positions (as parents, as academics, as middle-class immigrants, and so on). These positions then color our observations by allowing us only partial access to the field, by shaping the way in which our interlocutors interact with us, and by arming us with proto-theories of the world. These habits of thought are deeply ingrained in the ways we perceive the world and learn to think about it.

This does not mean, however, that we should assign primacy to fixed, generic identity categories as though we are working on an "academic paint-by-number landscape."[22] The danger here is to use these ready-made categorizations to obliterate the complex and multifaceted personal and professional lives of researchers and to essentialize them into a unidimensional stereotype. Positions are complex, situated, and often contradictory—involving the obvious race-class-gender trifecta, but also specific life histories and intellectual biographies. We may indeed see the world through gendered and racialized eyes, but we also see the world through the theoretical lenses of our training, political allegiances, and familiar theories.[23]

Abduction thus depends on the interplay of observations (the sign-object) and the way that the researcher's socially cultivated position—habits of thought and action—helps shape the interpretant. The disposition to perceive the world and its surprises in certain ways—including reflection on one's position in the world—is predicated on familiarity and affinity with broader theoretical fields as well as on the researcher's biography. If our goal is to provide a space for novel theorizations to emerge, we must recognize the crucial import of the scope and sophistication of the theoretical background a researcher brings along. Unanticipated and surprising observations are strategic in the sense that they depend on a theoretically sensitized observer who recognizes their potential relevance for the broader community of inquiry.

This view of abduction necessitates a radical shift from qualitative researchers' traditional reluctance to engage with theory, especially as such unwillingness has been formulated in grounded theory. Developing new theories depends on the researcher's inability to frame findings in existing theoretical frameworks, as well as on the ability to modify and extend existing theories in novel ways.[24] In-depth knowledge of multiple theories is necessary both to find out what is missing or anomalous in an area of study and to stimulate insights about innovative or original theoretical contributions. If we truly want to study swans (and whether or not they are white), we would do well to immerse ourselves in the biological literature on speciation and typology; if we want to study poverty in the inner city, we would do well to first immerse ourselves in the wide corpus of studies that have already addressed related questions—from ethnographic accounts to macro-structural historical treatises and quantitative studies. Rather than engaging with the scholarly literature at the end of the research project, as inductivist approaches have often advised, researchers who take abduction seriously need to have extensive familiarity with existing theories at the outset and throughout every research step.

From Theory to Theories

In-depth familiarity with a broad range of theories is thus critical for abduction, both in the acts of everyday theorizing and especially in more formal acts of theory construction. Any act that redescribes the world or presents a new narrative within it is a proto-theoretical abduction. And even a seemingly mundane conjecture, such as the one regarding a child falling out of bed, relies on previous proto-theoretical accounts. For an observation to become surprising, it needs to clash explicitly or implicitly with a vision of what the world should be like, how processes should unfold, and how actors should behave. Without such preconceptions, nothing can be either surprising or unsurprising; things simply *are* (to the extent that we can even distinguish events from each other, an act that also takes some proto-theoretical expertise). But to make the importance of theory generative for the research act, we need to further clarify what we mean by social theory.

As a way to approach this question, we take the pragmatist standpoint that a theory can be conceived as any form of generalization about observations that provides a potentially useful insight about the world.[25] *Useful* means that the theory extends its potential to future actions and understandings.[26]

There are, of course, different ways to generalize our observations.[27] For example, generalizations can articulate a set of heuristic assumptions about how people act in the world, or they can specify an ontology of the structure of the social world.[28] Theoretical perspectives such as interactionism, social phenomenology, and actor-network theory specify general assumptions about the way actors reproduce and change the social worlds they live in. These theories purport to tell us not what the world actually looks like, but rather what the structure of social action is. They explain the processes through which the social world is constructed and reconstructed. On the other end of the continuum, theories such as neo-Marxist accounts, institutional theories, and what Robert Merton once called "theories of the middle range" make claims about what the world is like. The theory, in this case, provides a substantive description.[29]

Both kinds of theories may inspire abductive inferences, but they do so differently. The more grammatical theories draw attention to unexpected meanings, experiences, or—in the case of actor-network theory—processes of enrolling technologies and people. Ontological theories, in contrast, let social scientists identify empirical anomalies that do not fit the predictions of the theoretical-descriptive mold.[30] For the purpose of stimulating abductive reasoning, our criteria are thus quite permissive: any generalized abstraction of the social world is useful as long as it inspires researchers by alerting them to an unmet expectation, and as long as it provides useful tools for abductively solving this anomaly. At the broadest level, it doesn't matter whether the theory generalizes by specifying the grammar of social action or whether it provides a substantive account of specific aspects of the social world.

Furthermore, the inspiration for abductive reasoning is not restricted to preexisting theories that have received an academic stamp of approval. The people whose lives we study tend to have their own explanatory frameworks. These may prove to be more illuminating and inspiring than academic theorizing. In that sense, the only criterion for useful inspiration is the general pragmatist guideline that theories are ways either to ask new questions or to make new observations possible.[31]

Stressing the importance of familiarity with theories does not imply a return to deductive theory testing. Knowing the literature and being intellectually positioned is far from coming to the field to verify, falsify, or modify a unified, firmed-up theory; it is still less finding only what we expect to find. Social research doesn't—and never did—provide a paradigmatic set of examples and ways to approach problems. There has never been only a single disciplinary matrix into which all knowledge fits, not even in the heyday of structural functionalism. In this sense, "knowing the theory" has always meant knowing the *theories*. Although researchers may be partial to a specific theorization, a specific theory seldom determines the scope of research findings.[32]

The necessity of engaging multiple theories also follows from semiotic considerations. As we argued in the last chapter, meaning-making is crafted in the dynamic relation among sign, object, and interpretant. Claiming that people approach observations with a single theoretical framework in mind would be simplistic. If this were true, the only way in which new abductive inferences would be possible would be in cases of resistance of the object. Although some social scientists seem to claim that this is indeed true, they do so by positing an untenable theory of action.

Imagine, for example, seeing graffiti in your neighborhood. As a street art connoisseur, you might be interested in the ways in which graffiti has morphed over the past decades, and in the kind of script artistry it embodies. As a social scientist, you might muse about the career trajectories of the artists, the ways in which the graffiti is a form of resistance to public propriety and aesthetics, and how it operates as an axis of distinction and status in a specific subculture. But at the same time, you might look at the graffiti and simply get annoyed about teenagers defacing your neighborhood and think fatalistically about property values. Interestingly, you may embody all these positions simultaneously, and the solidification of one interpretation over others is far from predetermined in the moment, but may depend on future interactions.[33]

Indeed, if we didn't occupy multiple positions at once, and if positions were not so internally complex, it would be a very boring world to live in: a world inhabited by one-dimensional actors who go around acting in all-too-predictable fashion, like characters in a second-rate novel. A multiplicity of positions and forms of possible action is crucial for understanding meaning-making in everyday life—all the more so in the act of social theorizing. In becoming social scientists, we usually explicitly learn to take on different theoretical positions rather than only one privileged way to understand our observations. As a glance at any syllabus for a contemporary social theory course would show, students' training is geared not to thinking through one privileged social theory but to gaining insight into multiple theoretical points of view, multiple ways to encase and generalize empirical observations. In this sense, the habit of action of the researcher is precisely that of thinking through different theorizations.

Abduction and Multiple Theorizations—An Example

To exemplify how a qualitative researcher leverages a varied theoretical base in developing theory, we turn to our own work, looking at how Iddo Tavory[34] theorized identification processes in his article "Of Yarmulkes and Categories." The wider context of Iddo's study was an ethnography of a Jewish Orthodox neighborhood in Los Angeles, in which he explained how Orthodox residents managed to sustain a religious life in the secular space of Los Angeles's Melrose area, known more for vibrant youth and creative subcultures than for Orthodox Jewish practice. Studying the neighborhood for five years, three of which he spent living there, Iddo became more and more fascinated by how experientially dense Orthodox neighborhood life was—how Orthodox residents were constantly "summoned" into interaction with other Orthodox residents, into participation in a plethora of Orthodox organizations, and into reminders that they were Orthodox Jews.

Thinking about how Orthodox residents in the neighborhood construct and sustain a religious way of life, Iddo began to delve into the literature on identity formation. Since the question of identity remains one of the core problems for any theory of action, the literature is vast. And yet two general modes of analysis emerged. On one side are strong notions of identity. In this reading, identity is a stable facet of the self. As people are socialized, they learn to occupy a position, which then becomes a constant force that pushes them to act in the world. If someone, for example, is an Orthodox Jew, identity theorists assume that the actor's actions would be largely defined by this kind of Jewishness. On the other side of the spectrum are approaches that find a constant sense of identity hard to defend. In this reading, identities, or rather "identifications," are interactionally emergent and situation-specific properties: there are no constant identities, but only situations in which certain membership categories are played out. Being an Orthodox Jew does not mean that there is a core identity pushing actors, but that Orthodox residents often find themselves in interactions and situations that elicit their identification as Orthodox Jews.

Although questions of identity and identification structured much of his work and reading, Iddo pursued other intellectual resources as well. He read urban sociologists to understand how neighborhood construction is described and to get ideas about how the neighborhood transformed into a religious destination. He also read ethnographic work that focuses on sustaining urban communities, which he hoped would provide him with comparative dimensions and parallel processes in other groups that he could draw on. Moreover, quite apart from his study, Iddo read pragmatist and phenomenological literature, interests he had since his days as a philosophy undergraduate and that he vaguely hoped would provide him with traction on questions of method and theory.

One of the breakthroughs in his research occurred when Iddo least expected it, when he was walking with an Orthodox friend on Halloween night:

> I walk down Melrose with Joe. We just got some tea at a kosher café, and are walking back. As we are walking down the street, a guy peeks out of one of the cars going east, he lifts the black Halloween mask he is wearing, shouts "Jews" and gives us the finger as the car zooms off. I am completely shocked. "Did he say 'you'?" I ask Joe. He laughs, "Jews." Joe sees my expression, and remarks "what, were you never called a kike before? It happens ... usually on holidays, when people drink and lose their inhibitions." I ask him if it happens a lot, "Not a lot, a few times a year, on the main streets. La Brea, Melrose. They never stop. Cowards ... you just ignore them."[35]

The incident was shocking on a personal level, but after the anger subsided and Iddo looked through his field notes more carefully, a theoretical puzzle emerged. The incident didn't fit neatly into either an identity or an identification theoretical framework. The abductive question "What should be true for the difference between Iddo and Joe to be a matter of course?"—or, in other words, "What should we assume in order to explain why they reacted so differently?"—did not elicit easy answers.

An identification framework, which treats identities as an interactional, emergent property of situations, seemed to take Iddo part of the way. When he was walking around with Joe, they were arguing about politics and gun control. There was no sense in which they were thinking about their Jewishness. If anything, Joe was talking like a libertarian-leaning Republican. In some sense, it was the anti-Semitic incident that made them into Jews in interaction. This seemed compelling: Jewishness emerged in the interaction, not as something fixed and stable. But there was a problem with such an abductive inference. If they were made into Jews in interaction, why was it that Joe, a young Hasidic man, could effortlessly orient himself to what had just occurred, while Iddo simply couldn't—he not only couldn't effortlessly orient himself, he couldn't believe he had actually heard the insult right.

So much for identification and the idea that identity categories are purely interactional achievements. But the opposite abductive possibility, presumed by the identity framework, didn't quite work either: neither Iddo nor Joe was thinking about his Jewishness. When Iddo asked Joe and many others in the neighborhood whether they thought about themselves as Jews when these things happened, he found that almost all of them could tell of regular incidents in which strangers noted and reacted to their Jewishness in everyday life—though rarely in an anti-Semitic register. People usually just wanted a sociable interaction and would ask them whether it was true that Jews believed this or that, or would tell them about their own religion. However, he was also invariably told that even though men sport a beard and a yarmulke, and women wear a head cover and a long dress, they often became oblivious of these garments as they go about their everyday lives. Although street interactions in which Jewishness became salient were common, the Orthodox residents were not constantly aware of their Jewishness in the sense of an identity that was constantly enacted.

Theoretically stuck, Iddo reconceptualized the problem. Instead of thinking of either identity or identification, he decided that the relevant question was how to explain different capacities to orient to such events—differing potentials for an activation of a category. This was closer to the actual observations, as the differences in the reactions were the immediate data at hand. Looking at this problem from the standpoint of differing potentials, Iddo gravitated toward the work of Pierre Bourdieu, who explicitly theorized his notion of habitus as the embodied and socially produced potential to act and react. But having the name *habitus* was not sufficient: to say that Jewish Orthodox people's habitus primed them to attend to their Jewishness when confronted seemed like a cop-out, a way to name a process instead of explaining it. Using *habitus* seemed to reify what happens, providing an air of academic sophistication rather than an actual theoretical account.

Shifting the analytical lenses proved useful in an indirect way. By moving from the question of identity and identification to potentiality, Iddo came to realize that a phenomenological tract he had recently read might provide the kind of leverage he found lacking in Bourdieu's account. The book was Aron Gurwitsch's *Marginal Consciousness*.[36] Gurwitsch, a philosopher who escaped to the United States with the rise of the Nazis, was influenced by Gestalt psychology, especially the notion that attention is always split between figure (what we focus on at the moment) and ground (the background, which we vaguely perceive, but which can potentially turn into the figure at will). When analyzing perception, however, Gurwitsch found Gestalt psychology incomplete. One of his most evocative arguments was that perception includes another crucial category—that of "marginal consciousness." Certain objects are on the margins of our attention, so although we do not attend to them, we can quickly reorient to them when a situation in which they are relevant presents itself. Learning to perceive, in Gurwitsch's account, is thus learning not only how to focus on a figure against a background, but also how to keep some things available even when they aren't perceived at all.

The notion of marginal consciousness, it seemed, could make sense of both the interaction Iddo began with and the other accounts and interactions he has since collected. Reading through his field notes, Iddo felt that marginal consciousness captured something important about his observations: what Orthodox residents learned was not necessarily to occupy an identity, but the ability to reorient effortlessly to situations in which this category becomes salient. This point struck him most powerfully when he found the following excerpt, which he had previously ignored:

Jonathan, Dov-Ber and I are walking back from synagogue on a Saturday. They are both wearing Hasidic garb, I wear a black jacket and yarmulke. As we cross one of the quiet residential streets, taking our time and talking about Jonathan's trip abroad, a car goes by, honks, and the driver shouts at us "This is Jaywalking!" Dov-Ber turns to Jonathan. "Did he say Jews walking?" Jonathan, shakes his head, "'Jaywalkers,' we were walking in the middle of the road . . ." Dov-Ber laughs. "Oh, jaywalkers."[37]

When faced with an unclear interaction—the car was going by, and the driver was shouting something—the first thing that Dov-Ber thought about was that his identity qua "Jew" was made relevant. Although the sign-object may have been vague, the interpretant seemed not only predetermined, but also ready to hand, practically at the tips of Dov-Ber's fingers.

Iddo theorized that rather than thinking of identification or identity, it would be much more useful to think about expectations and the ways people could call upon categories and ways of understanding that were held at the margins of consciousness. His article synthesizing these insights developed what he called "the phenomenology of interactional expectation": residents learned to reorient their Orthodox identification in interaction to keep this possibility on the margins of consciousness. These habits of thought and action meant that they didn't constantly perform their membership categories; they could expect others to evoke their identities. Whether they wanted to or not, they relegated the work of keeping the boundaries between the Jewish and the non-Jewish world to anonymous others.

This process could then be generalized not only to other Orthodox Jews, but also to people of color, women—anyone who expects to be called on as a member of a certain category. Indeed, other researchers have taken up this analysis as a resource for understanding race relations in Brazil or the predicament of gay soldiers in the United States.[38] The most surprising use of the article is in an analysis of the predicament of white supremacists in the United States. Kathleen Blee argues that right-wing extremists who begin covering their bodies with tattoos of swastikas and other white-supremacist script will come to expect people to reject them, make these inscriptions relevant, and treat them as white supremacists, whether or not this is the identification they are performing. Although the Orthodox Jews and white supremacists could not be more different, the social process is similar.[39]

Working through multiple theories helped Iddo in a number of ways. First, the original question arose through engagement with theories. The observation he started with may not have been particularly puzzling in itself. It only became puzzling in relation to the literature. Furthermore, the initial call for abductive inference was then modified through engagement with additional theories. By shifting theoretical lenses, Iddo could change the question as well as the set of answers that presented themselves. And through engagement with theory—both sociological and philosophical—he could then craft an abductive inference that would not only account for the specific observation he began with, but potentially also explain other observations and interview excerpts.

From Theories to Methods

In the last two chapters we began to map the relationships among Peirce's semiotics, abduction, social theories, and research methods. As Iddo's example makes clear, these elements all play a part in the construction of theories. They are crucial for our ability to recognize anomalies, to think about them creatively through different lenses, and to solve them in a way that makes for a novel and interesting new generalization. But as an attentive reader may also note, Iddo did not need Peirce's semiotics or his notion of abduction to conduct his research. Other qualitative approaches have also recommended that researchers enter the field prepared and well read. The extended case method aims at reworking theory by seeking out unexpected findings, focusing on the double fitting of theory and anomalous observations to provide theoretical momentum. And although Burawoy and others may be somewhat narrow in their preference for beginning with their "favorite theory,"[40] they otherwise construct their research program in a similar fashion. Does Peirce's pragmatism, then, simply amount to a way to remind qualitative researchers that they should be cognizant of multiple theorizations?

A pragmatist perspective, we believe, can fulfill its constructive potential only when extensive theoretical preparation is combined with systematic methodological data analysis. Multiple theorizations increase the researcher's ability to construct generative abductive inferences. They do so, however, only in relation to meticulous empirical observations and methodological routines. This, too, is obvious in the example—it was the resistance of the initial observation to some of the well-trodden forms of analysis that propelled Iddo to look elsewhere; and it was through variation and poring over earlier field notes and interviews that he gained some confidence in the budding theoretical direction. Rather than noting that theoretical promiscuity may be generative, we thus need to define how qualitative research can manipulate the relation between among sign, object, and the researcher's habits of thought and action—how it allows us to ask better questions by orienting the ways in which we look for answers. To do so, in the next chapter we begin to elaborate the pragmatic payoff for theory construction by examining how methods cultivate abductive reasoning.

4: ABDUCTION AND METHOD

Methods matter. If the contexts of discovery and justification are entangled, then the processes of gathering and analyzing observations become critical sites for developing new theoretical insights. Theoretical creativity is not simply a consequence of the accumulated experiences and theoretical toolkits a researcher brings to data analysis. Rather, data analysis as a methodological practice helps stimulate theory generation. Theoretical misfits do not automatically develop as we immerse ourselves in a research site or literature. Such misfits need to be drawn out through careful data analysis and an immersion in multiple theories. One important part of what makes the semiotics of the qualitative research process more systematic than our everyday acts of meaning-making is that in research we need to pay careful attention—far more careful than we usually do when we arrive at conclusions in everyday life—to observations in the field.

Meticulous field note writing, interview transcription, and systematic archival work help the researcher bring anomalous findings into sharper relief and thus open the grounds for theorization. So do systematically coding observations and writing memos on emerging insights. Why is this the case? Part of our argument in the last chapter is that although the methodological precepts of grounded theory methods are analytically powerful, they require rethinking in light of abduction. Here we are interested in what data analysis methods do for theory construction rather than in detailing the steps used in qualitative research.[1] We appropriate these coding methods from an abductive perspective in order to make them more analytically generative. We explain why these methodological steps matter for theory development beyond their obvious function as mnemonic aids and a means for increasing the phenomenon's resistance. Method is not the enemy of creative theorization, but its closest ally.

First Movement: Mnemonics

Qualitative methodologists usually present taking detailed field notes and making precise transcriptions as a check against faulty memory and the tendency to modify our remembered experiences so they fit better with the kinds of narratives we already want to tell. Although we think methods do much more, this remains an important point: as cognitive and social psychologists have long warned, selective recall and confirmatory memory biases are always looming. In a classic study of communication and rumor, Gordon Allport and Leo Postman showed people a picture of a subway car in which a white man threatened a black man with a razor. People were shown the picture, and then asked to tell about it to others. In some of the cases, when people told others about the picture, the razor migrated from the white man's to the black man's hand. Sometimes it did so on the second or third telling.

Similarly, the psychological literature regarding cognitive dissonance shows that when people have to act in a way that is incongruent with their prior narratives, their narratives tend to change. Thus, when students had to write a paper extolling the Cubans during the Cuban missile crisis, their opinions about communist Cuba changed: they could take the place of the Cubans in the crisis, could see things from their perspective. In another experiment researchers described a woman, "Jane," and provided a list of different behaviors she engages in, some of which were extroverted and some introverted.[2] They later asked people to assess whether Jane was a good fit to become a librarian. Not surprisingly, when they were asked to recall Jane's behaviors, they recalled the introverted behaviors better than they did the extroverted behaviors. In other words, people participating in the experiment remembered observations that fit with the way they imagined librarians should be (quiet, introverted people) and found it harder to recall observations that didn't conform to this image.

The similarity to field and interview recollections is clear. Even if we don't completely warp the past, we tend to remember the things that fit with our preconceived impressions of the site and truly not remember observations that don't fit as nicely. Although the object may afford resistance to its initial signification, it is often overshadowed by the interpreter's habits of thought and action. The resulting interpretant fails to take account of elements of the object. This, of course, is not a good idea if we want to conduct a study of librarians or of anybody else. In fact, if we are studying librarians, it might be more interesting to recall that Jane "didn't hesitate to speak with strangers when jogging" than that she was "shy and timid at the supermarket."[3]

Field notes operate as all methodological precepts do—they increase the object's potential to resist our interpretations. They make it slightly harder for us to say whatever we wanted to say before we came to the field. Although even while we are writing up field notes we have already made many proto-theoretical choices and have already screened some potentially valuable observations, it is still much better to record as much as we can than to have nothing at all. Similarly, a detailed transcription of interviews is important. If we do not produce close transcriptions, we will either change accounts retroactively or simply forget some snippets of conversation that could have proved crucial for our argument. Even if it is impossible to provide a full transcription that captures every utterance, movement, environmental stimulus, and biological parameter, this does not negate the aim of a comprehensive record. To appropriate Clifford Geertz's medical metaphor,[4] the fact that we cannot perfectly disinfect our scalpels does not mean we should conduct surgery in the sewer.

Methodological steps compel us to encounter the field again and again. We do this despite the fact that it is often the least immediately rewarding part of the research process. Writing field notes is a long and often tedious exercise, where the ethnographer spends as many hours at a desk as in the field, painstakingly writing down seemingly trivial observations. Ethnographers often do not want to go back and read through these notes; they think that they can use a few luminous observations that they remember well. They may also dread the encounter with their past selves in the field notes. Transcribing interviews is often boring, physically hard labor, and it is often embarrassing to hear all the missteps made in the interview, which is why researchers often try to pay someone else to do it.

Besides jump-starting analytical thinking, coding and memo writing also ensure that we thoroughly familiarize ourselves with our observations, that we do not forget the interactions we have been privy to once we put them down on the page. According to the precepts of grounded theory, researchers should expect to pore over field notes, interview transcripts, and archival documents to detect theoretical themes in a word-by-word, line-by-line, paragraph-by-paragraph, observation-by-observation fashion. This can be a slow process that takes place over the months, even years, that the research evolves. To underscore this point, Anselm Strauss gives an example of an entire coding session devoted to the first word of an interview fragment.[5]

Grounded theorists distinguish different forms of coding based on the unit and stage of analysis. Open coding takes the form of a brainstorming session where a researcher continuously asks what the observations could be an instance of and then further develops these ideas with additional questions.[6] If this is a conflict between spouses about child care, what is at stake? How do the partners bolster their case? Do they argue at particular times of the day or the week? What triggers the argument? What other factors are brought up during such an argument? In open coding, the questions may go in all kinds of directions. The answers to some of these questions will be in the observations, but other questions will require additional data gathering.

This open coding is followed by axial coding, where the researcher systematically examines a promising theme in the observations by looking across data sources to flesh out key conceptual dimensions and to account for variations. Rather than looking at one conflict, we compare several such conflicts across observations. Maybe some arguments between spouses are confined to child care, while in other instances the entire changed relationship with the advent of a child is litigated? Maybe married couples fight differently than cohabiting couples with children. Looking across interviews or observations on the basis of the kind of fight (contained or open-ended) or the kind of fighters (married or cohabiting) may explain the observed variations. Throughout this process, the researcher spins off theoretical memos and conceptual maps of the emerging analysis. Axial coding gives way to selective coding, in which the researcher theoretically works out one theme in a more formal theoretical way, such as a theory of the origins and consequences of conflicts between parents. Coding also prompts further data gathering when researchers notice that they want to double check the robustness of their theoretical ideas and make sure that they cover the common patterns and the exceptions. Coding activities thus span the entire course of qualitative research.

Taking field notes, transcribing interviews, and performing coding are important ways to guard against biased memories and the imposition of preconceived ideas on observations—in other words, to increase the resistance of the objects we encounter. And where field notes and transcriptions function as mnemonic devices, coding leads to greater familiarization with the researcher's observations. These procedures thus operate as methods of justification, helping the researcher to ensure that the path to the completed argument is not mired in incompetent memory and other cognitive biases. These practical processes do more than that, however. If we remain on the level of mnemonics, we divorce the research process from the active generation of theoretical insights and re-create the boundary between moments of discovery and moments of justification. A key point of a pragmatist position is that this neat division is untenable, that discovery and justification are analytically and practically intertwined.

Second Movement: Defamiliarization

To see how these methods help in abductive reasoning, we look more closely at the experience of transcription, coding, and writing field notes and memos—at both the phenomenology and the pragmatics of the research act. In order to get a better understanding of what methods do, we need to understand what methods feel like. Our argument throughout this chapter is that qualitative research methods do something more than provide the object with means of resistance. They allow social scientists to think creatively and to find surprises lurking in ostensibly obvious observations. In writing field notes, in transcribing, in coding, and in memo writing, we constantly objectify the world around us. From a stream of experiences we create a document. We then organize and reorganize this document: We highlight it in different colors and write various notes in the margins. We take different ideas and snippets and try to organize them spatially.[7] Our reading of the data prompts us to ask questions. We then return to the field to add observations and take stock again. In short, we subject our experience to all sorts of trials, which, as some researchers lament, render it quite far from the experiences we had in the field. Rather than lamenting the transformations of experience, however, we should celebrate these strategies precisely because they allow us to render familiar experiences alien, to defamiliarize our world.

The idea of defamiliarization[8] was best captured away from the social sciences, in the literary criticism movement of the early twentieth century known as Russian formalism. In a seminal essay the founder of the movement, Victor Shklovsky,[9] argued that poetics gains its potency from the defamiliarization of the language and experience of everyday life. In everyday life, Shklovsky contended, we tend to lapse into an automatic mode of action. To exemplify this idea, he used Tolstoy's diary. Tolstoy described how, while dusting his room one day, he suddenly realized that he couldn't remember whether he already dusted his sofa. The action of dusting had become so routinized that it couldn't even be remembered. Tolstoy, and Shklovsky after him, used the dusting of the sofa to represent the habituated life, a life in which things are so familiar that they lose their contours.

Caught between habits and creativity, Tolstoy and Shklovsky both argued for appreciating creativity. As Shklovsky wrote regarding Tolstoy's questionably dusted sofa:

> And so, held accountable for nothing, life fades into nothingness. Automatization eats away at things, at clothes, at furniture, at our wives, and at our

fear of war. "If the complex life of many people takes place entirely on the level of the unconscious, then it's as if this life had never been."[10]

This, for Shklovsky, was the life of prose. What art does—through minute description, through the use of metaphor, by taking an odd point of view, or simply through unnatural line breaks in poetry—is to force us to confront our everyday experience as unfamiliar and thus to gain a deeper appreciation for it. Returning to Tolstoy, Shklovsky quoted at length a story told from the point of view of a horse. By using this unorthodox point of view, Tolstoy rendered a surprising number of everyday things strange. For example, the idea of private property became problematized when the horse mused about how strange it is that people thought they owned him, other people, the air, or the land—things that the horse regarded as simply there.

Art, then, makes familiar things strange and allows us to reevaluate our habitual, or what Shklovsky called "automatized," nonappreciation of them. Art makes things the object of attention rather than of habituated action. In Shklovsky's words, art allows us to vividly feel an object; it makes "a stone feel stony."[11]

Shklovsky quickly realized that there are other ways in which the world can become strange.[12] The First World War, in which he fought, and life in the Soviet Union under Stalin were two such historical junctures. In these unpoetic situations, Shklovsky realized that nothing in life could be taken for granted anymore. Everyday actions took on special meaning: smoking felt different when every toke of a cigarette on the front line could be the last one in the midst of war. When saying the wrong thing to the wrong person might spell death or banishment to Siberia under the Stalinist regime, writing and speaking up became defamiliarized. In an uncanny way, everyday life came to feel unfamiliar.[13]

In pragmatist terms, defamiliarization takes an object that has all but ceased to offer resistance and problematizes its signification, turning it into a problem that requires a creative solution. Supplementing Shklovsky's focus on defamiliarization with a pragmatist viewpoint, however, forces us to slightly rework his position. As brilliant as Shklovsky's insight is, it seems to suggest a naive realist position regarding the relation between our perception and the world. In his schema, defamiliarization forces us to feel the phenomenon as it is, as if the stony quality of the stone were always there. Defamiliarization would then force us to experience this stoniness anew. This would mean that any poem about a stone (or a tree, or a loved one, for that matter) would make us experience the object in a preexisting way. If all defamiliarization does is force us to perceive the object as it is, then the best art can do is to highlight various previously existing aspects of the world.

In a novel and creative way, Shklovsky returns to the "the myth of the given": the view that knowledge of what we perceive can be independent of the conceptual processes that result in perception. If we think, in contrast, about defamiliarization through the prism of pragmatism, a more interesting picture emerges. In that case, defamiliarization forces us to encounter the object as a particular problem. The specific depiction of the object matters. The poetic depiction of the stone is understood as an opening that posits the stone as a particular kind of problem. Different poets present different problems, and different poems push us to construct different stones.

Translating Shklovsky's definition and effect of the poetic back into qualitative field methods, we make a simple first point: qualitative methods are not only mnemonic devices, but also ways to stimulate defamiliarization grounded in empirical materials. An interviewer reading over a painfully transcribed interview, for example, is often surprised to look at the objectified flow of conversation, at the nuances of turn-taking, or at the interactional process of creating a common understanding of what the interview is about. The interviewer realizes the missed opportunities to ask pertinent questions or the places in which the interviewer inadvertently obstructed the flow of the interviewee's narrative. But there is an important revelatory aspect as well. Snippets of talk that were almost invisible suddenly stand out; shreds of narrative that the interviewer took for granted during the interview come into sharp relief. Ethnographers are almost always amazed, when writing field notes, at just how much is going on in even the most mundane of interactions. This defamiliarized surprise is a necessary first step for abductive inferences.

This detour through Shklovsky and Tolstoy leads us back to semiotics and abduction. Defamiliarization, to use Peirce's theoretical language, is a technique that pushes us to question the relation between the sign-object and our habits of thought and action in producing an interpretant. By defamiliarizing the object, we can begin to ask questions that we simply wouldn't think of if we took the object for granted.

Here is one example. In an ethnography class exercise, we ask graduate students to write field notes about a visit to a grocery store. Most students start their notes with walking into the store and grabbing a basket or cart. We stop them and ask why the visit starts there. When and where to start a description is a critical research decision because it sets the stage for what is to follow. When does a visit to the grocery store begin? Is it in the midst of cooking, when we are confronted with an empty cupboard, soon after payday, or when we are driving past the store? Does the trip begin with a look through coupons mailed out on Tuesday evening, or does it begin with making a list of items to buy? If most students begin their field notes in a similar way, it is because the experience of grocery shopping has been understood as starting at that particular moment.

We then ask where that impression comes from. Is this the way grocery store owners like you to think that shopping begins? Do they like you to forget traveling to the store as part of the shopping journey? How, and when, do people become aware of different beginnings? Maybe when the grocery workers go on strike, when there is a gas shortage, or when there is a weather calamity. We keep asking questions. Where does the store begin? Does it begin at its automatically opening doors, on the sidewalk, in the parking lot, in radio and billboard advertisements? What zoning or other government agency regulates the beginning of stores?

Something as seemingly banal as going shopping for food can thus become analytically productive once we start examining the layers of assumptions that make shopping a seamless, taken-for-granted activity. One of the warrants for qualitative research is to defamiliarize those assumptions and examine how they are maintained.

Third Movement: Revisiting Observations

Abduction emerges from the relationship between multiple theoretically cultivated ways of seeing the world and the resistance of the object. Whereas theories allow us to initially see a phenomenon in interesting ways, methods are designed to first defamiliarize the field and then allow us to revisit the same observation again and again in light of new theorizations. As in any act of reading, methods provide the possibility to revisit the same text and find new meanings, as well as patterns and inconsistencies that we would miss if we did not objectify our experience in writing.

Thus a third function of qualitative methods in the context of theory construction stems from the researcher's revisiting of recorded phenomena in light of existing theoretical accounts. Of course, the act of writing down observations colors experience in the hues of textuality.[14] Insofar as notes, interview recordings, transcripts, and visual recordings evoke the observation, they will help us not only to reconstruct the experience but also to layer new experiences. Drawing on the work of philosopher Jean-Luc Marion,[15] we note that even without methods, "experiencing the phenomenon" should not be conceived of as a singular occurrence, sealed and done with after the first encounter. Rather, as Marion puts it, perception is always "saturated," that is, the phenomenon overflows our initial perception. In the stream of daily life we often revisit our experiences, and as we revisit them, we re-experience them in different ways.

FIGURE 3. Piet Mondrian: *Composition No. II with Red and Blue.*

FIGURE 4. Theo Van Doesburg: *Simultaneous Counter-Composition.*

One of Marion's examples of such an overflowing of a phenomenon is that of a man looking at a picture in a museum. Halfway into this visit, he suddenly finds that when he thinks about the picture again he understands it differently and sees things he missed when he was physically in front of it. This revisiting of the phenomenon is possible because as he walks around, the temporal change is followed by situational changes, and with them, changes in his proclivity to see things in specific ways. A good curator knows how to position works of art in a way that opens them to multiple readings as visitors move within the exhibit. The situational specificity of such experiential revisits allows us to position our perception in new relations to other phenomena, to case it differently at different points in time.

To take a relatively simple case, imagine visiting the Museum of Modern Art in New York and looking at the 1927 Piet Mondrian painting depicted in figure 3. Having walked through parts of museum already, you might first think about how minimalist the painting is—how little *there* there is. Perhaps you will think about how geometry and a bit of color can sustain an artistic effect. As you move away and continue to walk around the room, you might catch a glimpse of a painting by one of Mondrian's colleagues who led the De Stijl movement with him, such as the 1929–1930 painting *Simultaneous Counter-Composition*, by Theo van Doesburg (fig. 4).

Now thinking back on the Mondrian painting you just saw, you may be struck by the fact that Mondrian's pictures all use straight vertical and horizontal lines, only a few colors, and an abundance of empty white space. Van Doesburg uses similar straight lines and colors, but his paintings have a lot less empty space, and his lines go diagonally rather than horizontally and vertically. If you are a modern art enthusiast, you might know that these issues were heatedly debated in the De Stijl group (Mondrian left the movement partly because of diagonal lines). But if you are simply attentive, these differences will suddenly come to the fore as possibly relevant aspects of Mondrian's painting. The angle of the lines, and the amount of empty space, which might not have been as obvious on the first viewing as an important aspect of the painting, become so later, as you look at other paintings.

As Marion stressed, we live in a world of saturated phenomena. We are constantly reexperiencing parts of our world as we go about the business of living. When we move through our surroundings, we not only encounter new problem situations but find new problems in old situations.

To return to the research project, Marion's insight means that we will revisit our observations whether or not we commit them to writing. Observations that were not very "luminous" in the field[16] may become luminous as we think about them later—after, for example, we attend a stimulating talk and begin musing about our observations. Methods allow us to perform such revisits with more confidence. Field notes, photographs, and transcriptions can all be seen as contrivances for revisits. They are materially designed to ensure that our experience is revisited again. They take advantage of the ways in which the same observation changes as it is perceived at different points of time or from different theoretical vantage points.

In some sense, it may seem as though we are returning to the notion of methods as mnemonic devices. But there is an important difference. The idea of methods as mnemonics and resistance-increasing devices positioned them squarely on the side of the context of justification: methods were ways to make sure that our ideas were checked against the empirical. Instead, by treating field notes, transcripts, memos, and other forms of objectified evidence as sites for revisiting phenomena, we continue to position methods simultaneously within the contexts of justification and discovery.

Although there is no magic formula for theory construction, the complementary processes of defamiliarization and revisiting increase the possibilities of abduction when these processes take place in a context of existing theories. Defamiliarization makes sure that we mull over aspects we took for granted on the basis of our preexisting ideas and proto-theories, and revisiting allows us to case the same observation in different theoretical ways as we go along. Practically, in both coding and memo writing, researchers force themselves to take a relatively small data excerpt and work through it in detail in light of their theoretical expertise, trying to find as many possible ways to contextualize the observations as can be found. Each casing abstracts and highlights different aspects of the phenomenon, renders it comparable to different phenomena, and turns it into a concept that can then be linked to other concepts to form a theoretical statement.

As our perception of the phenomenon is colored by theoretical and proto-theoretical sensitivities, some of those encasings will fall easily within the realm of existing theories. Others, however, may be more difficult to fit. Although the literatures in which we are steeped guide the analytical process, careful coding usually means that imposing theory on observations is not that obvious. Working with observations in light of theories requires us to defamiliarize and revisit these theories. It may, for example, be initially easy to perceive a vague instance of stigma in a research situation. To ground such an observation as an example of Erving Goffman's theory, however, will probably require a close examination of a spoiled identity, interactional sequences, a social world of allies-in-the-known and others, and specified consequences of reassurance and friction. Careful coding almost inevitably requires further definition and operationalization of concepts, processes, and theoretical links.

Methods are thus codified processes designed to maximize abductive reasoning, in which we force ourselves to remain with the phenomenon and try to form as many links and hypotheses as possible in light of our theoretically positioned knowledge. To quote Peirce, the trick is to continue analyzing the observations word by word, line by line, paragraph by paragraph in order to "turn over our recollection of observed facts."[17]

Working with Observations: An Example

Very few published accounts of qualitative research provide the level of reflective detail that offers insight into the career of an original theoretical insight. When researchers write, they assume that people want to know what they found, and perhaps an idealized version of how they found it. They do not assume that people want to read about the false starts and dead ends, about what they had read just as they had their idea, or about the multiple attempts to provide a compelling theoretical account. Thus, although we have many celebrated original and theoretically inspired qualitative studies, they usually lack reflection on how empirical surprises stimulated new theorizing. The extensive literature of grounded theory–informed qualitative work remains, consistent with the tenets of the approach, cagey about explaining the role of existing theories in conceptualization. In addition, good abductive insights may seem obvious in retrospect.

A rare example showcasing the way observations and theory intersected in a research project is that of Diane Vaughan's historical ethnography of the disastrous space shuttle *Challenger* launch decision.[18] This disaster occurred in 1986 when the space shuttle exploded soon after launch, killing its seven crew members. Vaughan was initially attracted to grounded theory's emphasis on making constant comparisons across cases but explicitly qualified her use of grounded theory with the proviso that "we always have some theories, models, or concepts in mind."[19] Having already conducted three earlier case studies of organizational failure, Vaughan approached the *Challenger* case with a previously developed organizational theory of misconduct inspired by Robert Merton's theory of deviance. This theory, itself an amalgam constituted from multiple other theories, suggested an interplay among three sets of factors: forces of competition and scarcity that act as pressures to violate laws; rules and organizational structures and processes that present actors with opportunities to violate these laws; and a regulatory structure that systematically fails to deter such violations.[20] Vaughan initially intended to further strengthen her theory by selecting a new case that would allow her to elaborate it across various organizational forms. The report of the presidential commission on the *Challenger* accident seemed to confirm the initial impression of misconduct: its authors pointed to flawed decision making in which NASA managers and engineers knowingly took risks because of economic pressures.

The theorization of misconduct, however, did not fit neatly with the *Challenger* case. Vaughan kept finding disagreements in testimonies by engineers and managers that didn't seem to fit the narrative she expected. What outsiders saw as clear deviations from internal norms, Vaughan discovered was behavior that fit NASA's organizational culture. In one of the most striking breakthrough moments, Vaughan realized that the investigators and the engineers used the same language in different ways. Both investigators and engineers talked about "waiving launch constraints." The engineers kept repeating that the constraints were waived, and the investigators were incredulous and kept asking, "But how could you waive the launch constraints?" Vaughan's realization may seem at first to be trivial: after reading the transcripts for the umpteenth time, she saw that they used *waive* in two different ways. The investigators used *waive* as a verb; engineers used it as a noun.

As Vaughan read and reread the documents of the investigations, she found that the misunderstanding was consistent across her observations. Engineers repeated that they had performed "a waive." Investigators, in turn, remained flabbergasted. Vaughan realized that this mismatch was indicative of something much deeper. For investigators, talk of waiving launch constraints was a confession of misconduct. One simply does not waive such things. But for engineers, she realized, there was a procedure for waiving launch constraints. They followed a protocol constructed to authorize such waives. At issue, then, was a pattern of misunderstanding that investigators missed. If engineers followed a protocol, Vaughan realized, the entire case had to be theorized anew, because in that case there had been no misconduct.

Vaughan described the critical test she put this new insight through:

> To determine whether this case was an example of misconduct or not, I had decided on the following strategy: Rule violations were essential to misconduct, as I was defining it. . . . I chose the three most controversial [rule violations] for in-depth analysis. I discovered that what I thought were rule violations were actions completely in accordance with NASA rules![21]

Faced with broken expectations, Vaughan needed to change her interpretive framework of the kind of case she had. She had been carrying out a study of misconduct; now she shifted to explaining the *Challenger* launch decision as an action that stemmed from an organizational culture that normalized previously agreed upon forms of deviance.

In other words, it was the interplay of theory and careful investigation and transcription that pushed Vaughan to identify the anomalous observation and its import for analyzing the *Challenger* launch decision. One problem both the engineers and the investigators faced was that they had only a fleeting interaction to go by. As Vaughan carefully sifted through the observations, reading them again and again, the interactional mismatches that had been overlooked—the ways that investigators spoke across each other without even realizing it—came to the fore. As she revisited the observations, some aspects that had been neither luminous nor even visible became crucial. People often misunderstand and speak past each other in everyday interaction. They usually smooth over these possible mismatches and assume that they mean the same thing, and usually ignoring such mismatches allows the interaction to proceed smoothly.[22] By repeatedly looking at the transcripts of investigators' and engineers' conversations, however, Vaughan was in a better position. Taken out of its original context, the interactional flow of the investigation became defamiliarized enough for Vaughan to locate such mismatches.

At the same time, these mismatches were anomalous only in view of a theory of misconduct. After all, people often talk past each other without much consequence.[23] As with any abductive move, surprise emerged only through its relation to theory-driven expectations. It is only when we begin with a set of theoretical expectations about the way the phenomena we study should unfold that careful data mining becomes helpful; it was only through the theorization of organizational misconduct that the different ways investigators and engineers used the word *waive* became luminous.

This interplay of observations and theory then recursively reoriented Vaughan's sociological problem: Vaughan reconceptualized her observations as an organizationally produced *mistake* instead of misconduct. The story was one of the normalization of deviance that culminated in disaster, not of a single catastrophic oversight. By abductively positing an organizationally produced mistake rather than misconduct, Vaughan changed the lenses of her research in terms of useful theories and data sources. For example, she observed that in spite of holding different positions, managers and engineers shared a common worldview. To account for this observation, she dug into the literature on new institutionalism that explains the increased similarity of institutions over time though the creation of a common frame of reference brought to decision making. Simultaneously, this realization and the newly relevant literature prompted Vaughan to cross-check each individual's testimony, interviews, and actions as reflected in historical documents. In other words, the new literature led to more observations which in turn led to different theories.

At the end of her research, Vaughan theorized the NASA decision-making process as one of organizational conformity—a process in which gradually shifting local schemas of risk acceptability that are embedded in both professional engineering and managerial cultures, and that occur in an environment of structural secrecy, created an organizational process that normalized deviance.[24] She introduced several general points of view: The production of culture explained how managers and engineers gradually expanded the boundaries of acceptable risk. The culture of production referred to the macro-political and budgetary forces that normalized compromises between cost, schedule, and safety concerns. Finally, she highlighted an organizational structure of secrecy that allowed weak and mixed signals of risk to be routinized and filtered out prior to launch decisions, creating an impression that it was safe to fly.

From Observations to Variation

Data analytical methods are critical to stimulate theory construction and innovation. Rather than introducing new methodological steps, we have appropriated well-known qualitative research methods and demonstrated how they abductively facilitate theory development. Data analysis is not separate from theorizing. Of course, Vaughan did come to the field with an idea of what she would be looking for, and the idea proved to be wrong. By carefully revisiting a defamiliarized text again and again, Vaughan could put her ideas to the test. It was only after she read multiple investigations that the different understandings that investigators and engineers brought with them came to the fore. And then it was only after she put her idea to the test in the three most controversial cases she had that she realized that the anomaly in her observations meant that the whole theory of misconduct no longer fit her case. So far, so Popperian: the observation was used to refute a theorization.

What happened next can be captured neither by the notion of refutation nor by that of justification. Paying careful attention to her observations compelled Vaughan not only to reject her earlier theorizations, but also to move in new directions. She needed to rekindle theoretical expertise to see the anomaly in her observations. Once an abductive possibility emerged, she returned to her observations, now looking for new pieces of observations to pore over, new questions to ask. The theorization she finally settled on was the result of this recursive movement back and forth between observations and theories.

This recursivity highlights another aspect of the relation between theory and observations—one that we have so far sidelined in order to present the importance of observations and theory in qualitative research: working with observations is always working through variation of similar, different, and related instances. If Vaughan had found only one instance in which investigators talked past each other, if Iddo had found only one case in which an anonymous passerby reminded Orthodox Jews who they were, or if Fred Davis had found only one case of deviance disavowal, they simply couldn't have supported their conclusions. After all, if all they had was one simple case, the abductive possibilities would have been endless.

Imagine a less careful researcher in Vaughan's place, but one who has somehow arrived at the conclusions Vaughan had arrived at. Now imagine the following scenario: the researcher presents her work to an academic audience, telling this audience that, in one conversation she had looked at, investigators and engineers meant something different when they said "to waive," and then proceeding to present a theorization of the *Challenger* disaster. If the audience is at all attentive, the researcher's theorization will be torn to shreds. Perhaps the investigator was having a bad day? Perhaps the engineer under investigation was a renegade? In short, without recourse to variation, the argument wouldn't work. Without being able to show their audiences (and themselves) that what they found was consistent across different investigations, among different engineers, and over time, researchers simply can't make their case. But perhaps even more crucially, our thought experiment assumes that Vaughan's sloppy doppelganger could have arrived at the theorization without recourse to variation. This, however, is false. Variation not only helps us buttress a theoretical account, it is essential in constructing it. It is precisely through an accounting for variation that the theoretical object emerges. The next chapter thus focuses on variation and theoretical generalization. There, we ask what counts as variation and how variation is tied to theorization.

5: VARIATION AND CONSEQUENCES-IN-ACTION

We began chapter two with an example of abductive inference in everyday life: looking at a homeless girl accompanied by a vicious-looking dog, we wondered whether the dog might provide her protection in dangerous street life, or whether a dog might offer camaraderie when she is down and out. We recalled other cases of homeless people and their dogs, but in a haphazard way. In everyday meaning-making, we do not go out of our way to systematically think through different cases. When we encounter something out of the ordinary, we quickly come up with an abductive inference or ignore the encounter. And even though we may implicitly compare our observations to past experiences, and thus think through a rudimentary form of variation, we don't need to do so methodically.

In qualitative research any theory must account for variation. As researchers, we want to distinguish systematically gathered evidence from anecdotal impressions to create a compelling and empirically defensible theorization. However, systematically gathered evidence quickly accumulates into a mess of observations. We need to order this evidence to decide what kind of empirical and theoretical case we can plausibly construct from it. Ordering and making sense of observations entails an organization of cases — or, in other words, an examination of variation. But what kind of variation? And variation of what?

Variation denotes the differences and similarities among members of a preconstructed set.[1] It does not make much sense to proclaim that there is variation between the sun and a moose unless we assume that we are comparing them in relation to something they share (mass, or role in mythology, for example). Only if we assume a common question based on a theoretical premise that we can answer by looking at different empirical cases can we talk of variation. Variation thus depends on the construction of a set, a form of theoretically generated generalization. How is this set constructed?

To answer this question we must revisit Charles S. Peirce's pragmatism. We have previously outlined Peirce's semiotics and noted that he viewed meaning-making as the relationship between iterations of signs, objects, and interpretants. We argued that regardless of the topic or level of analysis, qualitative research is at essence a permutation of meaning-making in two ways. First, we follow actors' meaning-making practices. Second, qualitative research rests on puzzling out what kind of theoretical case an observation is—asking, in effect, how best to signify observations. We have then proceeded to show how methodology helps us manipulate signs, the resistance of objects, and our habits of thought and action. In order to offer an account of variation in qualitative research, we need to complement this semiotic picture with the pragmatist view of consequences-in-action.

In what became known as the pragmatic maxim from his 1878 article "How to Make Our Ideas Clear," Peirce argued that to understand or to get a fix on a concept is to spell out its consequences:

> Consider what effects, that might conceivably have practical bearings, we conceive the object of our conception to have. Then, our conception of these effects is the whole of our conception of the object.[2]

To understand the meaning of something is, in great part, to anticipate and examine its possible effects. Peirce did not intend the pragmatic maxim as the sole yardstick for clarifying ideas: he acknowledged that besides being consequential, ideas need to also be defined in other ways, such as with a dictionary-like definition and with a set of criteria that allow us to pick out instances of the phenomenon. Still, the pragmatic maxim was critical because if a concept or theory had no actual effects different from other concepts or theories (as Peirce regarded many metaphysical ideas in philosophy at the time), then it was useless for inquiry and deliberation.[3] If two concepts mean the same thing for all practical purposes, then what's the use in distinguishing them?

There is more to the pragmatic maxim. Not only is it valuable to examine the consequences of theoretical constructs, but the effects are also constitutive of the concepts. To understand that aspect of the pragmatic maxim, it is useful to turn to William James, who developed the maxim to refine his theory of meaning and truth.[4] In order to make the argument less abstract, James tells about a disagreement he was privy to. On a camping trip in the mountains, he came back in the evening to "a ferocious metaphysical dispute":

> The corpus of the dispute was a squirrel—a live squirrel supposed to be clinging to one side of a tree-trunk; while over against the tree's opposite side a human being was imagined to stand. This human witness tries to

get sight of the squirrel by moving rapidly round the tree, but no matter how fast he goes, the squirrel moves as fast in the opposite direction, and always keeps the tree between himself and the man, so that never a glimpse of him is caught. The resultant metaphysical problem now is this: *Does the man go round the squirrel or not?* He goes round the tree, sure enough, and the squirrel is on the tree; but does he go round the squirrel?[5]

The point James makes is deceptively simple: the heated metaphysical argument is meaningless. It centers on the question of what it means to go around. If *to go around* means to see something from all of its sides then, no, the man didn't go around the squirrel. If it means to circle an object while it stays in the middle, then yes, the man did. The point is that the concept of going around is defined in its practical outcomes. The argument is silly not because it is about a squirrel, but because the disputants assume that there is a self-sustained definition of *to go around* that precedes its practical consequences, rather than realizing that these practical consequences are part and parcel of the very definition of *to go around*.[6]

The pragmatic maxim helps us highlight two crucial aspects of specifying variation in qualitative research. First, the pragmatic maxim guides the act of theorizing variation: it provides a key criterion for evaluating whether we are on the right track with our concepts and theories. It can be used to examine the upshot of a theory, whether the theory has practical use, or more precisely, whether it potentially makes a difference in explanation. As Peirce came to see later in his work, a theory may have no current practical implications, but could still hold subjunctive implications if the state of the world would change. Thus consequences could be subjunctive rather than indicative. And yet, if all we can say about our theory is that it may make a difference if something that hasn't actually happened would, we are treading on very thin ice, which will probably give way with the first critical reader we encounter. The result would be too tentative to be useful.[7] The pragmatic maxim, then, offers qualitative researchers a means for evaluating the usefulness of empirically based theories.

Complementing the matter of definition and criteria, focusing on consequences has another upshot: it provides a methodological route to identify theoretically salient sets of variation. Peirce wrote, "we must not begin by talking of pure ideas, — vagabond thoughts that tramp the public roads without any human habitation, — but must begin with men and their conversations." Qualitative researchers dwell in these fertile habitats of conversations and actions when they construct concepts and theories based on empirical evidence to generalize and explain other phenomena. Through our observations we can follow consequences-in-action and bring these to bear on theorizations. Indeed, if "our conception of these effects is the whole of our conception of the object," we can abductively construct concepts from the effects we observe. When he wrote the pragmatic maxim, Peirce had experience-based effects in mind: "effects, direct or indirect, upon our senses."[8] Empirically following and mapping effects of people conversing, thinking, and acting allows us to build possible consequences into the genesis of concepts and theories.

Working through consequences-in-action is where variation becomes crucial: to work from consequences to concepts we need to systematically check a large universe of observations. Otherwise, it is hard to buttress the claim that the consequences we focus on really are consequences of the processes we conceptualize. In qualitative research, we thus study consequences-in-action that are constitutive of a theoretical case across observations. By thinking of observations as consequences within a semiotic framework, we have a means of marking theoretically interesting cases, and by tracing consequential processes of meaning-making we obtain analytical leverage to define and classify observations. Looking for variation then means searching for shared facets of semiotic chains that can be grouped into a set in a theoretically cogent manner, while differentiating them from those that seem dissimilar. And in the process of checking each new case for commonalities and differences, we come to redefine theoretical parameters.

An example will show the analytical payoff of using the pragmatic maxim as a methodological guideline. If we were interested in a study of racism, we could come up with a definition of racism and then code our observations for all instances that correspond to our preconceived notion of racism. In that case, our research consists of collecting evidence for a theoretical statement. We would get a sense of how common racist incidents are. Although this kind of definition is interesting and potentially important, it may be overly wooden and much better checked through quantitative methods.

When we are working from consequences-in-action, the meaning of our theoretical insights resides within their practical bearings. In the study of racism, we would ask ourselves: What are the consequences in the world that we call racism?[9] According to this view, racism is not simply *manifested in* hiring discrimination, in the reactions of police officers who assume that black people driving nice cars have obviously stolen them, and so on.[10] Rather, these practical consequences *are* racism. When we generalize, we then assume that there are additional theoretical consequences to the generalization we have produced, within or beyond our particular case. Similar to the way that pragmatism fuses the contexts of discovery and justification, it also fuses the testing of concepts and their theoretical meaning. With each new case added to a set, we redefine conceptual boundaries and theoretical scope.

This recursive relationship between theory and observations was nicely captured by philosopher of science Imre Lakatos.[11] Working on hypothesis-formation in mathematics, Lakatos observed that when mathematicians work through a hypothesis, they are necessarily exposed to diverse cases.[12] Some of these cases fall neatly into the theoretical framework the researcher started off with. Other observations, however, do not fit as snugly. The researcher's most interesting theoretical task is then to decide what to do with the latter cases. The researcher can simply say that these observations should not be considered in the study. Lakatos calls the strategy of refining a hypothesis in order to rule out nasty counterexamples "monster-barring." In monster-barring we decide that because an observation doesn't fit the theoretical mold, it is not part of the set and can be safely ignored. But the researcher can also change the theoretical scope of the research so that these seemingly exceptional cases now fit better as cases than as anomalies. Monsters, in other words, can be domesticated. The recursive relationship between theory and data is also the calling card of "analytic induction,"[13] an approach that rests on the assumption that anomalous data often change the theory, so that the *explanans* (the explanatory framework) and the *explanandum* (the observations explained) are mutually honed.[14]

In the context of abductive reasoning, the search for variation has additional value. This is because of two questions associated with the notion of abduction: Where do abductive insights come from? And how do we choose an abductive possibility from an infinite range of possibilities? We have already provided some clues for meeting these challenges: exposure to and familiarity with various theoretical traditions and with the methodological precepts of defamiliarization and revisiting, which help to stimulate abductive possibilities and aid us in sorting through them. Searching for variation by following semiotic iterations of consequences-in-action, however, constitutes the clearest strategy for getting traction within the research act on these dual challenges. Variation provides ample opportunities for the surprises that give rise to abduction. At the same time, the need to account for variation is the most important location in which possible abductive possibilities can be evaluated and culled: some generalizations are better at accounting for observed variation in the field than others. In short, the discussion of variation allows us to locate how theory and method mutually construct each other in qualitative research.

To recap, our aim in this chapter is to show how qualitative researchers may define a theoretical phenomenon of interest with a systematic exploration of variation. To specify the components of variation sets, we draw from Peirce's pragmatic maxim to conceptualize observations as consequences-in-action. If we are able to theoretically capture how iterations of meaning-making emerge in different cases, over time, or across situations, we import some methodological insurance against irrelevant theories. Examining differences and similarities among variations of consequences-in-action, along with double-fitting observations and theory, stimulates abductive insights when surprising patterns or outliers emerge.

Forms of Variation

We identify three forms of variation that qualitative researchers can use to recursively construct and test their theorization within a single case study, on the basis of the ways in which semiotic chains are constituted and morph over time.[15] The first is typical of most research, qualitative and quantitative alike. Here, we compare observations proto-theoretically understood as "instances of the same thing"—for example, teacher-student exchanges, the socialization of new army recruits, scientific collaborations, or people answering a survey question. The analytical point is to reflect on the axis that links the different observations as similar, or dissimilar, instances. Since this is the way most researchers construct datasets, we refer to this kind of variation as dataset variation.

The second kind, variation over time, takes advantage of the fact that semiotic chains are linked in time. Qualitative research often captures changing phenomena rather than discrete temporal points. The axis of variation is thus processual; the set is action over time: How do phenomena transform or remain the same as time passes?

The third form of variation, which we call intersituational variation, is the most complicated, but also the most creative from the point of view of theory construction. Intersituational variation takes advantage of qualitative researchers' ability to follow phenomena across settings and situations. Here we keep one semiotic element constant—whether signs, objects, or habits of thought and action—and follow it among situations. For example, rather than limiting ourselves to reflections on two aspiring lovers on their first date in a restaurant, we can follow these two people from the restaurant into their homes, their workplace, and their school classrooms to examine how the budding relationship ripples out into different settings.[16] When we look for consistency or contradictions across settings and time, observations that may not at first seem connected to each other become theoretically linked.

Dataset Variation

The most common way to think about variation in the sciences is by distinguishing the conceptual parameters of a situation and observing how the situation varies across observations within a dataset.[17] The situation can be abstracted in different ways: We can construct an ideal type and compare every consequent situation to this typical case. Alternatively, and far more commonly, we simply assume proto-theoretically that a number of situations are similar enough to warrant comparison. We construct a kind of semiotic gestalt in which we assume the shape of the entire meaning-making process, and then map the ways in which actual cases differ from this gestalt. This form of variation echoes the work of John Stuart Mill, who codified routes to construct the relation between variation and explanation, perhaps the most important in this context being "the method of difference," in which we observe similar cases and look for a crucial difference that would explain the variation among them.[18]

We can harness this approach for constructing a dataset and defining the phenomenon of interest, although with some important caveats. The distinction between our view of variation and Mill's method of difference depends on when in the research process it is time to look for similarities and differences among observations. For Mill, the set comes preconstructed and is aimed at making a causal argument. Researchers presume that variant cases have a different cause and search to find the smoking gun of difference. As we take a more deeply pragmatist view, the theorization becomes recursively defined through its elements over the course of the research. As researchers go through their observations, they reshape both their theorization and the scope of the cases that fit into the sets.

Second, if we take Mill's notion of difference as our benchmark for dataset variation, we can see why variation has traditionally been seen as the territory of quantitative researchers. Because quantitative work depends on a large N of cases, it allows for statistical calculations of differences. Qualitative research, on the other hand, is usually considered to involve "small N" methods, in which we talk to relatively few people, hang out in one or two field sites, or deal with a small number of historical events.[19] Of course, in spite of the apparently limited scope conditions of the research, any compelling abductive inference in qualitative research is based on an account of a large number of similar cases within the purview of the study.[20] In this sense, Mill's method of difference is useful for qualitative no less than quantitative methods. And yet because qualitative researchers do not generally rely on the random probability distributions that are so crucial for quantitative inference, the search for differences through which we can rethink our case takes another form. Instead of assigning probabilities to distributions to calculate the representativeness of a statistical finding, qualitative researchers look for odd cases, something stressed by researchers of all stripes— whether grounded theorists or practitioners of analytic induction or the extended case method.

Some of the most compelling evidence for qualitative research comes from observations of unusual interactions, of situations that break down, or of encounters that go awry. These observations are often deeply consequential for insiders and outsiders alike and stand out as red flags signaling the need for a theoretical understanding. They may occur because of a direct manipulation by the researcher, because "shit happens," or because of some structural reason that makes the ethnographers' interlocutors prone to such situations.[21] These include situations that put respondents in a double bind, face long odds, balance short-term gains against long-term losses, or simply seem completely out of character. Often, these situations require actors to make their usually implicit forms of meaning-making explicit, both for themselves and for others in the situation.[22] Even if the taken for granted is *not* made explicit, these situations provide qualitative researchers with a new situation that they can examine, a new interpretant that can be linked to other meaning-making occasions.

All three extended empirical examples we have outlined implicitly depend on such an understanding of dataset: Fred Davis collected instances of similar encounters between visibly handicapped individuals and people deemed normal; Iddo Tavory compared and analyzed interactions in which anonymous others identified Orthodox Jews on the street on the basis of ethnoreligious signs; and Diane Vaughan ended up comparing instances of engineer-investigator interactions following the *Challenger* disaster and the semiotic short circuits that ensued. In all three studies, then, the researchers gained explanatory power by showing that their theorization allowed them to explain different observations of similar situations, as well as to show why some observations would vary. In each of these cases, the phenomenon of interest came into sharp relief through an examination of its consequences, and the set was recursively defined and theorized through the analysis of such variation within the study.

The recursive relationship between set and elements implies that it is not crucial for qualitative researchers to begin with one rather than the other. Thus Vaughan began her research from a predefined set—a theorization of organizational failure in which the *Challenger* launch disaster was supposed to be an additional element. On the basis of her assumption of organizational failure, Vaughan expected to find certain empirical observations in her field. However, after realizing that her preconstructed set didn't explain observations within her case—the *Challenger* launch did not unfold as a case of misconduct—Vaughan needed to rethink the relation between theory and data, set and elements. Vaughan then opted to jettison the original set and reanalyze the *Challenger* launch case in its own right—creating in the process a new theoretical set that had new members (the variation within the *Challenger* launch study rather than variation based on her earlier studies).

In Iddo's example, the theoretical argument emerged in reaction to a striking encounter—an anti-Semitic incident. Although recognizing the incident as theoretically interesting required quite a bit of theoretical preparation—this wasn't an inductive theory that simply emerged from the ground up—Iddo began with a tentative data point, then looked for other observations in order to construct a set. The theoretical work was an attempt both to account for the unfolding of meaning-making in the particular consequences, and to address the question "What is this observation a case of?" If part of the theoretical intervention had to do with an account of process—and thus, as we develop below, with variation over time—an equally important theoretical challenge was to define a dataset of similar instances. This required Iddo to decide whether, for example, only negative interactions counted as part of the set, or whether much friendlier interactions with non-Jews on the street counted. He also had to decide whether only interaction with non-Jews counted, or whether interactions with anonymous Jews were part of the set. These are theoretical questions grounded in an examination of patterns of meaning-making—as the logic of each decision is based on theoretical considerations.

In both studies, theories provide tentative abductive pathways connecting observations and constructing a set on the basis of the researcher's ability to trace consequences-in-action. And in both studies, as the researchers move between theorization and observations, the set changes. Fine-tuning the set is not only a widening or narrowing of scope, but a change in what it is that the researcher explains. Although some of the initial theoretical impetus may remain constant in both studies, the theorization of the object is finally defined through consequences-in-action, and it thus changes along with the elements in the set. Careful attention to data, then, leads to a search for more relevant data on the basis of the emergent theorization. This double-fitting of dataset variation also structures the way researchers organize their work. To strengthen abductive inferences, qualitative researchers may want to actively look for cases that may challenge both the possible hypotheses they came to the field with and the framework they began with. Qualitative researchers should thus seek out variation among their cases. This search for negative cases is designed to ensure that qualitative researchers do not ignore exceptions and do not complacently stick with a theoretically defined set that does not fit empirical observations.

Variation over Time

The theoretical generalization that researchers construct in dataset variation accounts for the differences and similarities among cases within a specific time frame as they fit into a larger generalization that extends in both scope and time. A second form of variation in qualitative research emerges when we trace meaning-making over time. Here, we take our cue from the continuity of semiotic chains, with the interpretant of one iteration of meaning-making becoming the sign of the next. Qualitative researchers typically look at extended patterns of action: ethnographers describe the unfolding of action and tend to spend extended periods of time in the field to witness how paths of action are constructed; interviewers often collect life histories and other narratives and examine how elements are linked over time;[23] and historical researchers follow transformations over time as their data provides them with opportunities to see how their cases transform. Even short interactional moments have a temporal narrative structure. The focus in variation over time is a comparison of different moments rather than of different instances. Theory accounts for the processual unfolding of action in its consequences.

Drawing on the theoretical tools of historical researchers, qualitative researchers of different creeds are thus interested in the path dependency of trajectories, in the social structure of turning points, in tracing events over time, and in local narratives of action.[24] As Peirce's semiotics, the pragmatic maxim, and accounts of temporality all remind us, meaning-making is embedded in a temporal structure. Action always carries its past along as well as pitching toward a future.[25] Although dataset variation is often used in tandem with variation over time, the brunt of theoretical force often lies in explaining how action coheres over time. That is, variation over time assumes that the before and after of a given process make sense under a specific theoretical description.

Several examples clarify this kind of variation. The first is William Sewell's masterful retelling of the storming of the Bastille as the defining moment of the French Revolution. The thrust of Sewell's theoretical argument is that although historical events have important characteristics, such as a heightened emotional state and a shift in preexisting structural relations, it is only through post-factum interpretation that they become transformative events.[26] Thus Sewell argued that although storming the Bastille was a "major turning point" in the 1789 revolution, what made it into a transformative event—the symbol of the overthrow of the old regime—was not only the historically bounded occurrence but also the interpretation of the event later on by delegates of the third estate. Initially, the members of the National Assembly in Versailles greeted the news of the storming of the Bastille with solemnity, fearing that irrational mob violence would give the monarch an excuse for bloody repression. Their opinion changed when, in the next days, it became clear that the Bastille's taking actually convinced the king that the royal troops could not be counted on, and they were called back to the provinces. The members of the general assembly began to view the Bastille takeover as a necessary violent episode of people standing up against despotism. The assembly then took pains to distinguish the storming of the Bastille from subsequent instances of mob violence that threatened to engulf the nation.

In other words, what counts as an epoch-transforming event is a nego-tiated product of the meaning the event takes on later. To make this theo-retical point, Sewell showed that the storming of the Bastille was only one of a series of events, including the storming of another castle, riots in the countryside, and other acts that undermined the power and legitimacy of the king. In fact, the Bastille was attacked only after masses of Parisians broke into a garrison and took away thousands of musket rifles. Needing ammunition, they then turned to the Bastille, where gunpowder was kept. Although the Bastille was a prison-fortress that served as a powerful symbol of absolute sovereignty, no political prisoners were held there at the time— the freed prisoners were "four forgers and three madmen."[27] Thus, although in retrospect the Bastille became the singular event that defined the revolu-tion and even cemented the meaning of the term *revolution*, this was actu-ally an achievement solidified post hoc. The storming of the Bastille was not initially seen as symbolic of the overthrow of the ancien régime.

In terms of the logic of our discussion of variation over time, three issues stand out in this example: First, although Sewell was primarily interested in the explanation of action over time, he relied on dataset variation to make his case. He showed that there were other moments of agitation that could have been taken up. Thus even a theorization of process over time often in-cludes dataset variation. Second, dataset variation by itself is not enough to make the case. It is only when we trace the semiotic career of the Bastille's taking that the theoretical force of Sewell's description is apparent. Tracing the process as it unfolds through the eyes of both contemporaries and the following generations is the opening for abductive inference in this case. The generalization primarily takes the shape of an account of moments in a tra-jectory. Third, even this truncated example shows the theoretical richness of focusing on consequences-in-action to get a handle on theoretically relevant variation. Although the historical relevance of the Bastille assault seems indisputable and self-evident from our point of view, to contemporaries the issue was not obvious. Indeed, Sewell's point is to theorize how the event became consequential in larger historical narratives.

Variation over time is apparent not only in historical research. Ethnographic and interview studies are also, almost inevitably, interested in variation over time. This is most obvious in ethnographic studies of careers, which have been dubbed *becoming* studies. In these works—exploring the social process of becoming anything from a pot smoker, a boxer, or a modeling scout, to an opera fanatic or a religious convert—the theoretical account gains its potency from a comparison of moments in the process of becoming.[28] When does marijuana become enjoyable? When do people lose the emotional highs that follow everyday religious rituals? When do modeling scouts start to identify a potentially successful model from a lineup of young women who all have a very similar look? The role of abduction in all these cases is to account for the unfolding of the process itself. Taking advantage of the temporal possibilities of qualitative research capitalizes on one of the method's major strengths.

Variation over time also highlights the limits of focusing on instances that are obviously similar in ways we can predict at the study's outset. When qualitative researchers compare moments over time, these moments may at first seem quite dissimilar. The variation in observations is thus not a qualitative panel study in which the same indicator is compared at two points of time. This is not only because qualitative researchers attempt to follow continuous chains of meaning-making rather than disparate points in time, but also because the kinds of situations they observe as time goes by change as well. The challenges that a social movement faces in its first months, for example, are quite different from those one year later when the movement must decide whether to institutionalize a specific identity.[29] Looking at action over longer narrative arcs pushes qualitative researchers to consider what may seem like analytical apples and oranges. The next form of variation, intersituational variation, explicitly takes advantage of the diversity of observed phenomena: qualitative research captures not only variation over time but also variation in different settings.

Intersituational Variation

Intersituational variation is a logical corollary of dataset variation. Whereas dataset variation begins with the presumption that the situations we compare are entirely similar on conceptual grounds, the researcher's assumption in intersituational variation is that the situations are actually not similar, but that some aspect of meaning-making is similar enough to warrant inclusion in a set.[30] Here, the researcher collects actors'—and not necessarily the same actors'—actions in different settings and situations, and shows that seemingly unrelated actions make sense as a single set under the researcher's theoretical description. Thus in intersituational variation, theory explicitly takes center stage. The main challenge for other forms of variation is to convince readers that the theorization variation is cogent. In intersituational variation, the key move is to convince readers that the observations constitute a set, that there even exists meaningful variation. Examining structures of meaning-making as consequences in disparate situations, looking for commonalities and differences, offers a handle on this kind of variation.

Although this form of variation has rarely been analyzed as such, most good urban ethnographies—from Whyte's *Street Corner Society* to Liebow's *Tally's Corner* and Duneier's *Sidewalk*[31]—describe protagonists as they navigate different kinds of situations. To take a prominent example, one of the most important observations in Elliott Liebow's analysis of the fractured lives of inner-city black men is that they negotiated relationships with other men on the corner and with their female partners in different ways. The failed attempt to live up to a standard of masculinity gains explanatory breadth when we see the men bragging about their sexual prowess and manipulative attitude toward women among their peers and simultaneously witness how their relationships fall apart because they feel they cannot financially and materially provide for their female partners. Positing attempts to generate a competent masculine persona in the face of structural discrimination as his causal engine, Liebow could account not only for similarities among the actions of different people on the corner over time and in various employment situations, but also for how they made sense of their lives across situations, even if their actions at first seemed contradictory. What seem to be two very different forms of action became part of the same set, which we may term "negotiating masculinity in conditions of disadvantage." The abductive potential resides precisely in showing how the consistencies or contradictions of action across settings emerge and are linked through an examination of their consequences.

Except for relatively straightforward cases—where, for example, class position or personality structure are already supposed to affect a range of tastes or activities[32]—intersituational variation is virtually impossible to formalize because it groups heterogeneous situations into a set rather than grouping situations according to their proto-theoretical similarities. Theorization is explicitly what makes the different situations and observations comparable. Thus if we argue that there is a distinct "code of the street" that governs inner-city black men's actions, we expect to see such a code in action in other situations: in confrontations on the street, in job interviews, and in ways of seeing imaginary slights in mundane interactions.[33] This does not mean, however, that men would behave similarly in these diverse situations, but that it is precisely the diversity of the interactions that the theorization accounts for. Without the theory, the different observations are not obviously linked within a specific set in any way. As opposed to the sets constructed through dataset variation or variation over time, both of which may seem to proto-theoretically cohere, intersituational variation makes sense qua variation only through explicit theoretical engagement.

Intersituational variation, as an explicitly theory-generated form of variation, may take different forms. Our examples above have been of following one set of actors in diverse settings that do not seem at first to be part of the same set, except in the sense that they are connected biographically in their habits of thought and action. By the same logic, however, it is also possible to see how one setting has different uses, or to examine one set of signs in different contexts, or even to follow different people across different settings. In the most abstract terms, such theorization allows the theorist to move well beyond a specific field, looking not at a shared semiotic element but at the more abstract form meaning-making takes across situations.[34]

Variation in Communicating Newborn Screening Results

To demonstrate how variation is marshaled for distinguishing a theoretical phenomenon, we develop an example of abductive analysis in an ethnographic study. Here we limit ourselves to exemplifying dataset variation; in the next chapter we use the same case study to demonstrate the analytical power of variation over time and intersituational variation.

The study, conducted by Stefan Timmermans and Mara Buchbinder,[35] examined interactions between families and genetic teams following a 2006 expansion of a public health program of newborn screening in California. Within forty-eight hours after birth, a health care provider collects a blood spot after pricking the newborn's heel. The blood sample is sent to a laboratory, where technicians determine the concentration of specific chemical compounds in the blood. If the value lies outside a predetermined normal range, metabolic disease is a possibility and the child's pediatrician orders a follow-up test. If the results still suggest disease, the family is referred to a regional clinical center for further follow-up testing and, if indicated, treatment. The purpose of newborn screening is to use early identification to prevent the onset of diseases.

Positive newborn screening results are rare. Between July 7, 2005, and

April 30, 2009, the state of California screened 2,105,119 newborns. The program referred 4,580 newborns (or 0.22%) to a metabolic clinic for follow-up. Of those, 754 infants were diagnosed with a true positive. Expanded newborn screening thus identified one true positive screen for every 2,778 births. Of the infants referred to a metabolic clinic, 3,334 were not confirmed to have a disorder. The false positive rate for newborn screening was thus one false positive for every 633 births.[36] Although metabolic disorders are rare, their potentially life-threatening consequences render the results deeply influential.

The study focused on the implementation of expanded newborn screening to identify infants with metabolic disorders early enough that parents and clinicians could take action to prevent the devastating effects of the disorders. The analysis was primarily based on observations of clinical interactions between parents and the genetics team—which consisted of four medical geneticists, a nurse practitioner clinical coordinator, a dietitian, and a social worker. The ethnographers followed parents during clinic visits over a three-year period (October 2007–July 2010). In the metabolic genetics clinic, they audiotaped consultations between parents and genetics staff with a research team member present to observe the interaction and take ethnographic field notes. In addition, they attended weekly staff meetings, consulted patient records, and interviewed families in the home and in the clinic. The families of seventy-five patients participated in the study.[37]

A Puzzling Incident

We'll start with a puzzling interaction about the meaning of screening results. Stefan entered the patient room with a geneticist, Dr. Silverman, who told him beforehand that the patient—four-month-old Michael—was picked up by newborn screening for a rare condition called medium chain Acyl-CoA dehydrogenase deficiency disorder (MCADD), but that the screening result was likely a false positive. The geneticist planned to discharge the family from the clinic during the visit. Because most families hope for a healthy child, he expected the meeting to go smoothly. Instead, several interactional misfits occurred.

In the small patient room, the geneticist found a family of four. Strollers and diaper bags took up much of the space. The mother, Sarah, held her talkative two-year-old daughter in her arms while the father, John, had Michael sleeping in his lap. After short introductions, the geneticist mentioned the purpose of the visit. He prefaced the conversation with: "You know that one of the down sides of [newborn screening] is that it causes great anxiety. False positives cause great anxiety. So, here's what the original thing was: you had two abnormal metabolites." Dr. Silverman explained that those elevated metabolites indicate two diseases, GA1 and MCADD. John interrupted: "What is GA1?" The physician replied: "Glutaric acidemia type 1. And that—" John interrupted again: "And so is this something new, that?"

The geneticist attempted to clarify: "No, it was there right from day one of the newborn screening. Now that's not a great condition to have. Although, the truth is that when we have remodel [that is, retest] cases, they may be noncases." When the father protested that he had never heard about GA1, the physician tried to reassure him that MCADD was their major concern. When he went over the follow-up testing results for MCADD, he concluded that Michael was probably a carrier for the disease. He said, "Do you know, probably one in forty people or one in thirty people are carriers? And it's not a big deal." Sarah, however, started to cry, sobbing: "But it's children who might have it."

Dataset Variation: Diagnostic Uncertainty

From both the clinician's and the family's point of view, this interaction takes several unexpected turns. The clinician anticipates dismissing the family from the clinic as likely false positives, while the parents expect an update on follow-up test results that hopefully will give Michael a clean bill of health. The parents are surprised that Michael has screened positive for two conditions when they have been told only about one. The physician does not understand why the family reacts so emotionally to what he anticipated would be good news to them—that Michael is likely only a carrier for MCADD and not affected with the condition.

The components of the semiotic process are easily apparent in this interaction. The critical target of signification is the newborn screening results (the signs), which, according of the physician, indicate an out-of-range value for two conditions (the object). The reaction in the interpreters or the interpretant is surprise, alarm, concern, and worry in the case of the parents and a belief in a likely false positive for the physician. The parents' reaction becomes a new sign leading to a new interpretant in the form of frustration for the physician. The physician reacts then with more explanation about the frequency of carriers in the population, which does not have the desired effect when the mother burst out in tears (another interpretant for her and simultaneously a sign for the physician).

What are these consequences-in-action indicative of? The situation is messy. We only have a strong sense that something went quite wrong. The question, however, is whether this is a random event that can be written off as an emotional overreaction due to miscommunication or whether the interaction is typical of a kind of newborn-screening physician-patient en-counter. In the latter case, the hunch is that something in the way newborn screening is set up generates these kinds of consequential reactions. A strik-ing observation prompting dataset construction thus does not necessarily need to be typical; it may also be an exceptional instance suggestive of a pat-tern. Either way, the observation could become an element in a set, and the analytical work is to create this set.

Even when researchers start with a luminous observation, they can go in one of two directions: they can look at other observations or turn to the literature for inspiration regarding the kind of case they have. In reality, re-searchers often do both in quick order.

In this instance, the researchers turned to the medical sociology litera-ture on uncertainty.[38] This literature is tied to the question of whether uncer-tainty produces a dogmatic attitude among medical practitioners. The con-cept of uncertainty has played a central role in medical sociology scholarship in addressing the question of how clinical knowledge is acquired and utilized in medical education. Renee Fox argues that medical knowledge is inher-ently uncertain both because it is riddled with gaps and unknowns, and be-cause the number of medical facts is ever expanding and impossible to com-pletely master.[39] Fox's sociology of medical knowledge stresses a gradual acquisition of medical confidence: instead of blaming themselves for clinical mistakes, aspiring doctors learn to successfully manage the limitations of medicine. Training for uncertainty imprints a professional attitude of objec-tive expertise and detached concern on the next generation of physicians.[40]

Other authors have questioned the primacy of uncertainty and instead highlighted that "training for control" closely follows "training for uncer-tainty."[41] They note the learned dogmatism of medical practice and warn against an overconfident medical attitude centered in technique and disre-garding patient-based notions of health and illness. Although most social researchers—and also most medical practitioners—agree that the medical knowledge base is marred by uncertainty, scholarly disagreements persist about whether technological innovations foster scientific skepticism or a dogmatic attitude. These opposing approaches to medical uncertainty be-come apparent in different communication styles with patients.[42]

This literature offered a theoretical vantage point from which to situate the observed interaction. The recent expansion of newborn screening based on multiplex technologies also offered a benchmark for when prevention is wanting. Researchers learned that parents expecting clear answers from screening are thrown off when the positive results raise questions about the presence of a previously unmentioned disease and when questions about the presence of disease remain unanswered. Uncertainty thus seemed a useful analytical theme for looking at this data incident. Yet questions remained about the kind of uncertainty the ethnographers witnessed: How prevalent is this kind of uncertainty in newborn screening and for the parties who experience uncertainty? What are the consequences of uncertainty?

The layering of the existing literature, combined with the accumulated observations, suggests a set—interactions in which the emergence of uncertainty is the main axis of comparison. To get firmer analytical traction on the elements of such a set, the researchers needed to put it in a series of similar interactions with uncertainty as the axis of differentiation. Across the observations in the study, they created a database of similar interactional units of analysis, of parents meeting with clinicians to discuss positive screening results, to see how they varied on a spectrum going from uncertainty to certainty of screening results. This dataset of variations could then be used to determine whether uncertainty emerges in all or only some situations, whether there is one predominant kind of uncertainty, what the consequences of uncertainty are, and so forth.

Looking across the patient visits, it became clear that parents varied in how seriously they took newborn screening results. John and Sarah's reaction of shock, urgency, and danger was the dominant response in clinic visits. And yet there were some exceptions; not all parents took the possibility of hidden disease seriously. There was also variation among agreements and disagreements between clinicians and parents. The situation in which parents responded to the newborn screening results as an emergency while clinicians tended to offer reassurance was common, yet for other cases parents did not seem to take the condition as seriously as clinicians did. These variations are all located among interactions of obviously similar situations: the initial reception of the news and the doctor-patient interaction that ensues.

The process of abductively double-fitting observations and theory now began in earnest. The major line of scholarship on uncertainty—Does an uncertain knowledge base make clinicians dogmatic or humble?—did not capture the salient characteristics of the interactions between parents and clinicians. Situating the interaction between Michael's parents and Dr. Silverman among many other similar interactions shows that the uncertainty experienced was of a diagnostic nature. A diagnosis may be thought of as a cognitive schema that offers a plan of action for both patient and clinician. Patients typically present physicians with a number of complaints, signs, and symptoms to be organized into a clear-cut diagnosis.[43] When the diagnostic process does not lead to an established disease, the cognitive roadmap suggesting treatment plans is lacking. Diagnostic uncertainty typically takes the form of determining whether symptoms warrant a disease classification, but, as the clinic interaction showed, it can also include uncertainty about both the presence and nature of a medical disorder. Diagnostic uncertainty is particularly vexing in the case of newborn screening because the infant is asymptomatic and cannot express discomfort. The only indication of disease is thus the screening results. When these results are ambiguous, uncertainty prevails about what to do and whether disease is even present.

With rare conditions added to the screen, the question facing clinicians is not only whether the baby has a disease but also what the nature of the disease is. On the basis of a close analysis of the data, Stefan and Mara argued that informing patients of a positive screen without clear criteria of what constitutes disease turns the newborn into a *patient-in-waiting*.[44] This is someone kept under close medical supervision even though a diagnosis remains elusive. A dataset of forty-two out of seventy-five families experienced a patient-in-waiting situation. The uncertainty about what to do and whether the child is actually sick created anxiety among parents. The observed interaction between Michael's parents and Dr. Silverman is one of a set of recurring instances in which the introduction of medical technologies generates a new form of patienthood due to diagnostic uncertainty.

Situating an event in a series of similar events helps us to abductively define what kind of general phenomenon we are dealing with. The set of interactions carved out of the clinic visits illustrates the recursive nature of abductive analysis in a way that was different in the Vaughan and Tavory examples: a focus on diagnostic uncertainty dislodges uncertainty as a practical problem for clinicians alone to one affecting a broad array of involved parties and highlights the functionality of diagnosis within medical bureaucracies. These theoretical refinements, in turn, lead to new ways of ordering the data. The meaning of newborn screening is thus traced through careful attention to actors' chains of meaning in action. In other words, by following semiotic chains of a similar kind of interaction, researchers provide a generalizable account that specifies the theoretical link between observations of different families.

Our approach shows the added value of following the pragmatic maxim in data analysis. If we had started with an official definition of what newborn screening is and then looked for indications of such a definition, we may have dismissed our observations as noise or reclassified them as inevitable side effects. By focusing on the consequences of newborn screening for the presumed beneficiaries, however, we could argue that diagnostic uncertainty partly constitutes the meaning of the program: "Newborn screening is what it does."[45] Following consequences-in-action allows us to bracket the presumptions of normative policy discourses to define the program. The meaning of newborn screening is thus traced through careful attention to actors' chains of meaning. In other words, by following semiotic chains of a similar kind of interaction, researchers provide a generalizable account that specifies the theoretical connecting tissue between observations of different families.

From Variation to Explanation

Theory construction gains momentum when we situate an observation within a broader set of phenomena by examining its similarities and differences with other members of the set. In qualitative work, fitting data within sets is a recursive process that helps elucidate the common theoretical grounds of the set and the definition of our theoretical object. In other words, generalization depends on the content of the set: adding elements forces us to specify the conceptual boundaries of the phenomenon under examination, and often to redraw them. Examining such commonalities on semiotic grounds helps to reduce the messiness of observations.

Generalization and variation illuminate the pathway to theorization. The missing element from our working definition of *theorization* as "a generalization that accounts for variation," however, is what exactly we mean by "accounts for." To strengthen an emergent theorization we need to explain, rather than merely indicate, a clustering of similar phenomena. In the next chapter, we push abductive analysis to answer questions of causality. Positing the structure of meaning-making as our organizing analytic tool allows us to move to processual, mechanisms-based explanations and causality. Continuing with the example of newborn screening, we focus on how tracing meaning-making as consequences-in-action structures the research project, the search for causal explanations, and the researcher's ability to reject actors' own interpretations, as well as to deepen the explanation by examining underlying causes.

6: CAUSALITY

We have focused on research-driven theory as a variation-based generalization of observations. Multiple forms of variation allow researchers to craft an abductive generalization that fits observations by specifying common grounds of elements in a set, in relationship to a theoretical framework within which they are comparable. The process of double-fitting theory and observations then leads to an articulation of the kind of case we have. This minimalist account of "theory as generalization," however, misses perhaps the most coveted aspect of theorizing: explaining why observed events occur. A compelling data analysis not only moves from observations to an abstracted description, but also provides readers with a causal explanation of variation.

Moving from variation to causality may seem like an unfortunate step. Causality, as many have observed, is a philosophical minefield.[1] As the eighteenth-century philosopher David Hume famously argued, causality is, by definition, invisible. We can never see causality—what we see is ongoing changes in the world, and perhaps we recognize some regularities in our observations over time. Upon these observations we then impose a causal structure. In the language of Immanuel Kant, causality is a category of human reason. Moreover, any causal account ignores much of what is happening, providing an overly neat narrative that highlights only what we see as essential for the story. As John Dewey stressed, causality is a logical "slicing" of a continuously changing and complex world, a temporal stream in which cause and effect as regular occurrences that neatly follow one another in time may be abstracted[2] but can never be clearly separated.[3]

And yet focusing on abduction and meaning-making in action already presumes causality. In its most basic form, abduction asks what we should assume to be true to render a surprising observation "a matter of course," as Peirce put it, implying a sequencing of events influencing each other. Intimately connected to this idea, the definition of meaning-making as iterative semiotic chains that are built on one another also presumes that one iteration of meaning-making shapes the next. Thus, although it may be true that researchers impute causal relations that are invisible, this is an empirical challenge rather than an intractable philosophical dilemma.

The focus on the unfolding of meaning-making in action makes for a specific approach to causality. Blowing over from medicine, where the randomized clinical trial prevails, experiments have increasingly been elevated as the gold standard of causality, even in the social sciences. This interventionist approach, however, captures only one possible form of causality. Indeed, philosopher of science Julian Reiss notes that various working definitions of causality exist in the social sciences.[4] Besides interventionist causality, Reiss distinguishes between counterfactual accounts, regularity accounts, and mechanistic accounts. Reiss then notes that each kind of causality is compatible with particular forms of evidence and disciplinary aims. For example, econometricians tend to treat the notion of causality as synonymous with prediction, and for many "large N" researchers causality is a matter of establishing regularities over time. Our discussion of variation already subsumed rudiments of a regularity-based causal logic, as we look for multiple cases and their variation to buttress our case. It also presumes an elementary form of counterfactual thinking: when researchers are refining the scope of variation, they inevitably wonder what would have resulted if this or that aspect had not happened, and they look for such variations across cases.[5] But these are, at best, complementary accounts of causality in qualitative research.

What, then, is the causal niche of qualitative research? Because of qualitative researchers' strength in capturing unfolding meaning-making processes, we hold that causal explanations based on qualitative evidence are most amenable to mechanism-based accounts. This form of causality gains its explanatory power by tracing how a social phenomenon came into being or how it acts, and it does this by looking at its underlying structure.[6] In an influential essay on mechanism-based causality, philosophers Peter Machamer, Lindley Darden, and Carl Craver define mechanisms as "entities and activities organized such that they are productive of regular changes from start or set-up to finish or termination conditions."[7] Mechanism-based accounts assume that explanations can be decomposed into parts and their actions to specify generalizable processual links. These links then show how an explanandum continuously leads to an explanans. Importantly, mechanisms gain explanatory power when processes occurring on a lower order of aggregation explain how something was produced on a higher level of aggregation or abstraction; the level at which a causal mechanism must work is irreducible.[8] Indeed, as sociologist Neil Gross observed, "All work on social mechanisms assumes that mechanisms are the gears in some social machinery and thus stand in a relationship of lesser to greater vis-à-vis the causal effect they bring about."[9]

The level of aggregation deemed low enough in a mechanism-based account depends on the kinds of problems a discipline tends to contend with. As Machamer, Darden, and Craver argue, every scientific discipline has a relative "bottoming out" of lowest level components constituting the elements for mechanisms. Looking for such elementary building blocks, researchers constructing mechanistic explanations in the social sciences have mostly relied on rational choice theory and other individual-based theorizations such as bottoming-out components.[10] After all, they argue, what can be more "fundamental" than human choice? But these individualistic reductions, as many have argued in different contexts, are not as straightforward as their proponents suggest. Assuming essential and presocial human nature and social action is problematic: people may act reasonably, but reason itself is defined socially and emerges interactionally.[11]

Drawing on pragmatism and especially on Dewey's work, Gross has made the case for moments of social action—problem solving in social practice—as alternative foundational processes in mechanism-based explanation for the social sciences. Gross rightly assumes that the kinds of explanations social scientists look for are necessarily grounded in human action and, often, reflexivity. Gross's pragmatist account of social action leads him to define social mechanisms as "composed of chains or aggregations of actors confronting problem situations and mobilizing more or less habitual responses."[12] Centering attention on habitual problem solving appropriately shifts the unit of analysis in the mechanisms literature to the moment of action, along with its situational and socially emergent features, without making untenable assumptions regarding human nature and rationality.

The notion of habitual problem solving, however, has its limitations as the bottoming-out level for a qualitative approach to mechanisms. Whereas mechanisms need to provide an intelligible language through which causal processes take place, the focus on problem solving leaves a key question unanswered: How exactly do people solve problems? Gross emphasizes that meaning-making is central to the pragmatist theory of action; in fact, he says that a "mechanism is interpretive all the way down."[13] And yet Gross's focus on habits as forms of social and epistemic culture and resources for action bypasses the pragmatist-semiotic theory of meaning precisely where it might be of most use. Focusing on habits and thought and action, Gross ignores the crucial importance of the sign-object in shaping the interpretant. By focusing on the structure of meaning-making, qualitative researchers are poised to provide precisely the kind of intelligible and continuous mechanism-based account that is irreducible to other levels of aggregation. In other words, abductive analysis lends itself to causal explanation because of its dependence on tracing semiotic chains of meaning.[14]

Working through variation by examining consequences-in-action as we did in the previous chapter already provides us with the beginnings of a causal explanation. Because we define phenomena by following semiotic chains over time, we already have ideas of a phenomenon's explanatory narrative flow in terms of the sequences of meaning-making it is made of. By comparing observations to each other to find similarities and differences, and by trying to see whether they recur, we then develop a pattern of meaning-making processes that we can account for with a theoretical argument. In producing a set, we already make claims about the beginnings of causes and the unfolding of action.

However, because we focused on variation as a way to define a theoretical phenomenon of interest, we de-emphasized the role of mechanism-based causal accounts. To better illustrate the power of a mechanism-based processual understanding of causality, we revisit the newborn screening study. Our goal is to explain the variation observed among parents' reactions to a positive newborn screen that produced diagnostic uncertainty. By attending to the semiotic chains varying across cases, we are able to explore four different explanations: a social science explanation of the observed variation as a patterned semiotic structure; research subjects' own explanations; an alternative explanation found in the social science literature; and an account that goes beyond the initial observed variation to point to a deeper underlying causal explanation. As we do so, we show how abductive analysis can help researchers both construct and cull causal accounts.

Reaction to Frameless Situations

In the previous chapter, we proposed that a phenomenon of interest is the recurrent experience of diagnostic uncertainty affecting parents and health care providers of a newborn with a positive screen. What explained this diagnostic uncertainty? Across the entire study, the most revealing pattern of variation between cases was the recurrent interactional misalignments between clinical staff and parents. In some interactions, parents and clinicians tended to be in accord about the status of the child, while in others they disagreed, and this led to interactional standoffs. The stakes were high for clinicians and parents living under the specter of a possible metabolic disorder: if the condition was real, intrusive and costly interventions may be necessary to prevent mental retardation or sudden death. The proposed explanation accounting for the variation in the study highlights parents' and clinicians' reaction to the absence of an interpretive disease frame. How does one evaluate a situation in which a child is potentially ill, but shows no symptoms, and may never have any symptoms? This situation is uncharted territory, in contrast to the familiar frames of illness and health for patients and medical personnel.

The notion of framelessness that the researchers arrived at builds on Erving Goffman's theory of frame analysis.[15] Goffman posited that frames are basic experiential building blocks that guide the perception and interpretation of reality. They allow people to identify and label an infinite number of corresponding events. Goffman considered in passing the role of situations in which "reality anomically flutters,"[16] and the tendency to interpret such situations on the basis of existing frames, but he was more interested in how such frame breaking was socially organized and could be manipulated. Still, engaging Goffman's writings can elucidate the analytical dimensions of framelessness.

Taking the lack of a common frame as the key element in a causal explanation, we can account for the pattern of dataset variation: the situations in which parents and clinicians are in accord were those in which parents and clinicians agreed either that a child was already symptomatic for a condition, that the test results unambiguously confirmed the presence of disease, or that the tests clearly established a false positive screen. In these cases of agreement, the frame was one of disease or health, and both are frames that people know how to act on and align. But having a child with a positive newborn screen for whom the follow-up tests do not conclusively confirm a disease is much harder. When there is no actionable frame for a diseased-but-now-basically-healthy status, parents tend to fall back on the frame of the child as diseased, while professionals gravitate either to a likely-false-positive understanding or to a carrier understanding.

The differences in meaning-making between clinicians and parents stem partly from incorporation of different sources of information. Ironically, part of the reason that parents tended to embrace a disease frame was because clinicians initially impressed upon them the urgency and danger of metabolic disorders, which was further confirmed when parents checked online or printed information. For clinicians, however, the information available online and in textbooks was no longer accurate. They shared experiences via professional email lists and conference meetings with geneticists, and the as-yet-unpublished consensus was that newborn screening revealed that metabolic disorders are different entities from what was known before. The diseases are more common, have greater variation in severity, and may require different treatment approaches. But clinicians didn't know for sure that there was nothing to worry about with the infants identified in the early days of newborn screening. Their hunch was that some newborn screening patients require a new interpretive frame, but during the observed interactions they lacked the tools to construct a new interpretation. Still, they tended to be more reassuring than alarming for the patients with ambiguous results, especially in conversations with colleagues. The study thus captured a period of biomedical uncertainty in which existing epistemic frameworks no longer fit the signals from the screening program, and geneticists were gravitating to a new understanding while parents held on to the familiar frame of disease that clinicians initially provided to them in an attempt to prompt them to take the test results seriously.

This explanation of parents' buy-in to the medical frame was further confirmed when the researchers examined an exceptional negative case. A salient aspect of the observations was that almost all parents went along with geneticists in framing their child as potentially sick even when no symptoms were apparent. An exception, however, was a white middle-class father who suspected that the geneticists were experimenting on his child, who, in his opinion, looked normal and behaved normally. He expressed anger with the geneticists for needlessly worrying him, and he refused to commit to follow-up testing. Resistance against medicalization is common in health social movements[17] but except in the case of this father, it was absent in the newborn screening study. This exceptional reaction underscored that a frameless definition is not by itself indispensably causal but requires additional conditions to lead to diagnostic uncertainty.

The frame absence and misalignment explanation accounted not only for the variation between physicians' and parents' accord and discordance across the sample but also for variation over time and across situations. Some families experiencing diagnostic uncertainty resolved their initial discordance and came to agree with the clinician after the genetic test results offered definitive proof that the child was disease free. Other families, however, held on to the disease frame even after clinicians exhausted follow-up testing. Why would parents continue to treat their infant as diseased while the clinician was willing to declare the child healthy? The reason was that there was no authoritative test to clear the uncertainty. Instead, clinicians based their conclusion on the time that had passed without onset of symptoms. The parents, in contrast, ascribed the lack of onset to preventive measures they had undertaken to keep their child healthy. They resisted giving up on the disease frame precisely because the preventive measures seemed to be working. For clinicians by this time, the preventive measures were unnecessary. Hence, continued discordance.

The theoretical explanation weaves a generalization with an explanation about specific chains of meaning-making in action. The process can be summarized as follows:

1. Doctors and patients enter an interaction for which there is no readily available frame (people enter frameless interactions).
2. As they try to understand the situation, they fall back on available frames of illness and health (in interaction, people manage frameless situations by falling back on available typifications).
3. These frames are further reinforced by the sources of information available to parents and clinicians and the presence of authoritative clinical tests (resources serve to strengthen available typifications).
4. These frames fail, usually increasing the uncertainty and interactional failure observed in the field (because common typifications do not anticipate the progression of the frameless situation, interactional misalignments, and in this case diagnostic uncertainty, emerge).

The proposed causal mechanism thus rests on the reaction of parents to the absence or presence of a culturally available disease frame when their child tests positively for metabolic disorders. When kids are considered sick but are completely asymptomatic, the causal process evolves on the basis of the sources of information available from clinicians, the internet and media, and follow-up tests. With Gross,[18] we could consider these interpretive frames as habits, but by decomposing the semiotic sequences of the clinic interactions we are able to provide a more fine-grained causal account of the conditions under which habits of thought and action become relevant and emerge—as in the physicians' growing realization that the infants identified by screening differ from familiar patient populations.

Actors' Causal Accounts

From the perspective of some hermeneutic theories of meaning, the social science causal claim may be alarming. Some social scientists have interpreted Geertz's hermeneutic observation that qualitative researchers mainly tell "stories about stories"[19] as a license for blurring the difference between local actors' causal accounts and social science explanations. Instead of constructing dense explanations from actors' first-person interpretations of the situation, our theoretical account imposes an interpretation that differs from actors' own explanatory narratives.

Rather than beginning with interpretations, the current explanation begins with actors' *failure* to align their interpretations. According to the pragmatist perspective we develop here, however, as long as the ethnographer carefully attends to actors' semiotic chains, the researcher is not limited to the ways people interpret their own predicament. Like the ethnographer, actors in the field attempt to understand their circumstances causally, very often in generalized terms. If anything, the stakes are higher for actors—these are, after all, their lives. Yet ethnographers are not beholden to these indigenous explanations as final arbiters of causality. Although such explanations always count as observations in the sense that they constitute a sign from the field, they may not hold up as generalizable causal claims. We show this point with an elaboration of the newborn screening field notes.

In the last chapter, we outlined an ethnographic situation in which geneticist Dr. Silverman told Sarah and John that their child Michael was likely a carrier for MCADD and had indications of a second disease. The geneticist expected the parents to fall into a health frame, but the parents embraced an illness frame. Following this incident, Michael's parents brought up their own explanation for their reaction to Dr. Silverman's announcement. When the ethnographers interviewed the mother at a later date, she explained that Michael was a very different child from his sister, especially in his eating habits. An MCADD metabolic crisis is preventable if parents feed their children at very close intervals. If they become sick and begin vomiting or develop diarrhea, they will have few reserves to compensate for the lack of nutrition and may enter a fatal metabolic crisis. The clinic staff had impressed on Sarah and John the importance of feeding Michael at two-hour intervals, and Sarah found similar admonitions online.

With most infants this is not an issue, but Michael refused to eat. His birth weight was six pounds nine ounces, but it dropped to six pounds within a week. Sarah spent her days feeding Michael: "I was charting how many poops he took a day. How many wet diapers he had a day. How many ounces [of food] he had a day. And it was awful. . . . I can't even tell you. I think I have twelve different types of [bottle] nipples. . . . I couldn't enjoy him because every second I had, I woke up around the clock every two hours to feed him. . . . I kept my cell phone next to me, and I just set [the alarm] for every two hours." She visited the emergency room three times before Michael turned eight months, concerned that he was not eating enough. The consuming work of keeping her son fed also strained her marriage.

Sarah introduced a very different causal account that made her son's condition fit MCADD: her own brother had died at seven months from "feeding difficulties." An aunt of her husband had also died at a young age. Her son's diagnosis with a genetic metabolic condition pointed to possible biological continuities between relatives. In light of the family history, his feeding troubles could have indicated a symptomatic manifestation of MCADD.[20]

Sarah's explanation for the uncertainty that she experienced thus rested on the observation that Michael was different from his sister and on a family history of possibly fatal but undiagnosed metabolic disease. At this point

Sarah had an explanation on which she was acting, but that does not mean that we had a social science explanation. It could have been that families who experience uncertainty in the aftermath of newborn screening have suspicious family histories that render the screening results plausible, but at this point we only had a single moment in time within a single case. In order to buttress or reject this causal explanation, we needed to look at whether it would hold beyond the specifics of this incident. As it happened, variation occurred over time, which led to a rejection of Sarah's original causal explanation.

Although during the clinic encounter each party only partly grasped the other's perspective, the signals conveyed and picked up during the interaction were consequential for the outcome of the clinic visit. Rather than dismissing the family from the clinic, Dr. Silverman agreed to conduct DNA analysis for the most common MCADD mutations. This molecular test could provide conclusive evidence of Michael's carrier status. He decided to keep following the family until the test determined whether his hunches were correct. Michael's molecular results came back negative. At that point, Michael was considered disease free, a result the parents accepted.

Subsequently, in a follow-up interview, Sarah revised her previous explanation: "We've just kind of chalked it up as he's not a great eater." Rather than suggesting a medical tie between Michael and her deceased brother, she now linked her son's eating habits to her own picky eating: "You know, I am a small woman. I'm not even a hundred pounds. And I was a really poor eater, my Mom said, as well. So, we kind of just think he's just not a good eater. And now I can relax a little bit because it's not fatal if he doesn't." She also noticed her son's developmental milestones: "Michael was really good. He rolled over when he was five days old. Like his motor milestones, he met. Social milestones, he met. It was deceiving." The genetic test results shifted Michael from being a worrisome "bag of bones" into a healthy, maybe even precocious child with a difficult appetite.

Following Sarah's reasoning over time allows the researchers to reject its causal implications by tracing its consequences-in-action. If we were to generalize Sarah's account, we would assume that parents' reaction to being told that their child is a carrier of a possible genetic illness is primarily caused by personal histories of possible undiagnosed metabolic illnesses, comparisons between children, and observable behavior congruent with symptoms. This explanation seems straightforward until we examine variation over time. Although Sarah understood her situation through her personal history and her comparison of her two children, once her son was pronounced false-positive (and thus healthy) she did not simply abandon her past, but rather invoked a new past with a new moral: she now understood her son's eating problems as those of a picky, small, and precocious child taking after his mother. This, also, is a personal history, albeit a completely different one.

Rather than offering a causal account about why parents react as they do, personal histories play a different role. When parents struggle to understand the frameless situation of "patients-in-waiting," they fall back on either an illness or a health frame. In most situations, both these frames can be connected to past histories. Much like people's social positions, personal histories are complex, containing resources that fit both illness and health. Looking at variation over time pushes us to see such personal histories not as a primary causal factor for anxiety and uncertainty, but as resources for elaborating upon the frame they fall back on. Rather than functioning as a causal agent, they operate more as a vocabulary of motive—providing ways to make sense of one's own reaction in a situation, rather than the reason for the reaction.[21] Personal histories are flexible resources that can fit both illness and health. Sarah's methodical feeding and trips to the emergency department demonstrated the consequences of frameless situations being redefined as cases of illness.

Following semiotic chains and using them to construct axes of variation solves a methodological-cum-ethical conundrum: Can ethnographers produce arguments that work behind the backs of their subjects? Do researchers' explanations draw on actors' first-person experience, or do they construct "third person" accounts that are detached from actors' understandings of their situation? Our pragmatist approach implies that ethnographers can and sometimes should construct causal claims that seem very different from those the actors hold, but that these should meet a high evidentiary threshold. This threshold is met when they collect data and analyze it in systematic fashion for agreements and differences across cases. Ethnographers cannot simply assume, a priori, that they know better than their subjects do. Rather, the onus of rejecting actors' causal claims depends on an explanation's ability to account for variation.

Culling Alternative Explanations

Reaction to frameless situations is not the only way to explain the variation of responses to a positive newborn screen. Other explanations based on the social science literature are possible. One common sociological perspective is that concern about infants is specific to social class.[22] Working-class and impoverished parents, for example, may face more pressing issues and are more skeptical of medical information. They may also be more fatalistic and accepting of their children.[23] Middle- and upper-class parents have so much invested in their children that the possibility of disability is deeply alarming and upsetting.[24] Such a hypothetical alternative explanation builds further on the literature on how parenting differs by socioeconomic status.[25]

Genetic metabolic disorders affect poor and wealthy alike and thus form a good case to examine differentiation in response along class lines. In our study sample of seventy-five families, we found two small clusters of five to seven families who were less concerned than others about a positive newborn screening result. These clusters did not coincide with a defined social group. The first group consisted of some of the Hispanic families. They all encountered a geneticist who spoke only elementary Spanish or relied on a translator during the interaction. The reaction of the Spanish-speaking families who met with a native-Spanish-speaking geneticist, however, was more in line with the responses of English-speaking families—thus causing us to reject a "cultural" explanation. This result suggests that the first geneticist was simply unable to communicate the possible ramifications of the positive newborn screen to the families. Indeed, follow-up interviews with several of these families confirm that they had only a sketchy understanding of newborn screening.

The second cluster of exceptions was a heterogeneous group of families who already faced serious challenges, such as parenting an older child with a disability or dire financial problems involving jobs and housing. These families prioritized other consuming challenges over a positive newborn screen that presented only the possibility of disability in a newborn. Here, a class component is definitely present among families facing financial struggles, but we also encountered cases of impoverished agricultural workers who decided not to return to work so they could take care of an affected child. Some of the families with an older child with a disability, on the other hand, were solidly middle class. Rather than supporting a causal explanation grounded in class, these two clusters highlight the resources needed to respond to a positive newborn screen: a physician who is able to communicate with parents and the absence of other pressing concerns requiring immediate attention. This variation is thus a consequence of available resources, only some of which are economic; the default pattern is for parents to take newborn screening results seriously.

An examination of the variation along class lines also shows that the reaction of parents to newborn screening results is not a fundamental manifestation of varying socioeconomic resources and social capital. In fact, evaluating this alternative hypothesis provides further support for the critical role of diagnostic uncertainty because it locates some of the seeming exceptions in relationship to the dataset. It is impossible to prevent a positive newborn screen by mobilizing economic resources, and the uncertainty about what, if anything, is wrong with the child deeply affects parents across the socioeconomic spectrum. Parents of a child with a positive newborn screen who worked in medical professions and had correspondingly high incomes, for example, did not react differently to the news that their child may be affected with a genetic metabolic disorder. However, their exhaustive searches in medical databases may have put the diagnostic unknowns into sharper relief.

Causes behind Causes

Even though we rejected actors' own explanations for their reactions and addressed an alternative explanation found in the literature, the social science causal account for diagnostic uncertainty stayed close to the observed interactions. Our explanation of frameless interactions singled out a characteristic of the communication process between clinicians and patients. This is as it should be—the test of an explanation is how it fits the observed variation across cases when we retrace semiotic chains and consequences-in-action. Some social scientists, however, put a high premium on explanations that go beyond observable causes. They are interested in the invisible levers that set the causes within observations into motion.

The possibility of extending causes is a product of an explanation's narrative form. If a causal explanation is best conceived as a narrative, with a well-specified beginning, middle, and end, then an important part of the process of establishing causality is settling the question of beginnings. Many debates about alternative causal claims relate to our point of departure, or our "emplotment"[26] of stories. Do we begin the story of the French Revolution, for example, with the rise of the Enlightenment ideas, with the political and economic rise of the bourgeoisie, with the uprisings of peasants in the countryside, or with the construction of the storming of the Bastille as a profound change in the rules of political engagement? Such decisions, as pragmatists and others have noted, are crucial in shaping the contours of the story we tell because they push us to ask different questions about the organization of the field we study.

The promise of revealing such invisible causes behind causes is one of the most appealing aspects of the extended case method. Whereas a grounded theory approach inevitably sticks close to observations, the extended case method gives researchers license to link observations to structural macrosocial forces, even if they are largely unperceivable in the research project. Instead of assuming that conflicts in Zambian mining towns, for example, reflected only local interests, early anthropological extended case studies situated these conflicts in a context of growing urbanization with village-city conflicts and in a history of colonialism. Thus they extended their cases in both time and in space.

Where the initial anthropologists were not careful enough, and where kindred sociological theorizations of method followed, was in the assumption that researchers can know in advance what kind of historical or inter-situational causes are important and what kinds of explanatory extensions are warranted. The danger of the extended case method is that there are no methodological checks and balances on invoking those macro-theoretical forces and mechanisms: the smallest interaction may become emblematic of global sociopolitical collisions with little articulation of mediating processes.

In other words, construing underlying causes becomes problematic when it seems to relax the research's evidentiary standards or revert to a dogmatic theoretical stance. As we move farther from empirical materials, we risk losing the methodological testing of recursively double-fitting theory and data and may thus be misled. Those methods, after all, make it difficult to impose unchecked explanations on data. The challenge of abductive analysis is to extend the case without relaxing methodological standards. The solution is to stick to empirical explorations of causes behind causes, relying upon additional observations.

We can make this causal exploration only *after* we have ascertained the most compelling explanation with an examination of variation. The test of the historical deepening of causality remains whether or not these causal explanations are situated within chains of meaning in action we have found in our initial observations. The links between the condition the researchers want to deepen and the historical context they mobilize should be conceived of as a part of the research—not as its context or background. Expanding the scope of an explanatory theory may thus require pushing beginnings back in time or extending the causal field to conditions currently invisible to the researcher. In turn, we may need to revise our theoretical abductions because new data-theory misfits have emerged.

In the newborn screening study, for example, we may want to examine how the initial shock that parents experienced when they were informed of the screening results follows from the process by which newborn screening was institutionalized. Parents in the study were usually unaware that their infant had been screened because in all states but the District of Columbia they did not consent to the procedure. The infant was usually screened as part of hospital or birthing center discharge procedures and consent was implied. Parents may have received a brochure with information but little further explanation. There was thus little phenomenology of beginnings, and no attempt to set the new medical frame with the blood draw.

In a time of fears about "genetic discrimination," privacy concerns about biological samples, and political debates about government involvement in health, why do we have a quasi-mandatory screening program without consent procedures? The program of newborn screening started with screening for phenylketonuria (PKU) in the 1960s, a time of limited awareness of informed consent.[27] PKU happened to be an ideal candidate for screening: if parents became aware that a child had the disorder, early dietary intervention promised to prevent mental retardation.[28] In subsequent years, several authoritative medical bodies reviewed the possibility of genetic population screening programs, using newborn screening as an example. When bioethicists began to argue for informed consent in the 1980s, newborn screening proponents justified the lack of informed consent by emphasizing the public health benefits of screening entire populations for rare conditions for which early identification could lead to prevention of significant disability. In the meantime, however, many disorders had been added to the screen for which the health benefits of screening were more ambiguous; for example, it is not always possible to prevent the onset of debilitating conditions, and for some adult-onset conditions knowing at birth is not critical. Still, an infrastructure that was put in place decades ago created obduracy against change. The lack of informed consent and accompanying conversations about what results parents can expect[29] still affects the shock parents currently experience when they are informed of newborn screening results. This lack of consent for newborn screening and education about it during prenatal medical visits also stunts the possible development of a newly shared frame.

With this historical deepening, the researchers linked diagnostic uncertainty to decisions made fifty years ago when the first newborn screening programs were implemented. They also linked it to a series of institutions that could have modified consent procedures for newly added conditions—and thus perhaps would have helped create a new frame—but refrained from doing so. There are several implications of this historical move on the part of the researchers.

First, once again, the researchers went beyond actors' interpretations to distinguish causes. Second, they rendered invisible causes visible rather than postulating the causes. At no point in the ethnographic research did any clinician or patient make even an indirect reference to the historical implementation of the screening programs. The institutional path dependency was thus invisible. The only indication was an absence: the remarkable fact that U.S. states gather blood from more than 99 percent of infants without asking parents for consent. Although these causal extensions were ethnographically invisible, they remained empirically traceable, and they dovetailed with the work of historians of genetic screening.[30]

Third, the excursion into the history of screening programs generated a theoretical opening. In addition to engaging theoretical writings about interactions in a clinic, the causal extension to the 1960s may require engagement with a diverse literature on institutional decision making and the scholarship on health social movements. Our challenge now is to theoretically accommodate both the institutional path dependencies and the interactional framelessness. This, in turn, provides a new question linking Goffman's analysis of experiential frames to institutional arrangements, and looking at the path dependency of experience.

Fourth, tracing the causes deeper into time tends to produce more tenuous causal explanations. We are now tracing back single storylines rather than a cluster of varied observations. This does not need to be the case, as researchers could look for variation among different public health and medical interventions, some of which require informed consent, and look for common institutional decision-making trajectories. Of course, if they followed this path, the researchers would end up with very different projects.

Finally, the beginning of this causal explanation may still seem somewhat arbitrary:[31] the researchers could have gone even farther back in time and asked where screening programs came from or when people started to think of diseases as distinct entities located within bodies. Where do we stop? What project should we have? A pragmatist approach provides a useful heuristic for such questions because it views research projects as answers to practical concerns. We have to think back about the relevance of our project: if our goal is to understand observed diagnostic uncertainty, it may not be necessary to retrace the history of diagnoses. We can take for granted the medical assumption that the biochemical values of blood may indicate disease. On the other hand, if we notice, for example, the emergence of radically different conceptions of disease etiologies in the screening program, then we may need to follow that history after all.

Variation and Causality

Qualitative researchers have been reluctant to engage in causal arguments. Causality, however, is ubiquitous though implicit in grounded theory's emphasis on social processes, extended case method's search for social forces, and other approaches' focus on mechanisms and explanation. In fact, we have rarely come across qualitative research that doesn't implicitly make causal arguments, even when its authors carefully avoid the word. Some of the reluctance to make explicit causal arguments has to do with the untenable logical standards of causality as necessary and sufficient conditions to be established experimentally, as with the search of some researchers for overarching, timeless "covering laws."

Our sense of causality, instead, draws from the pragmatist maxim: as phenomena become apparent through their consequences, we can trace these consequences back at least as far as their immediate causes. We find a processual approach useful because we hold that the social world is necessarily one of shifting patterns of action, where no single pattern can completely explain an outcome, and where no single characteristic is sufficient for explanation. Delineating single causes sacrifices too much external validity for meager analytical payoff. As we work through variation to establish causality, we also gain traction on some of the stickiest problems of qualitative research—the status of our interlocutors' interpretations, and the extension of explanations over time.

As we argued, when we focus on consequences-in-action, we are not limited to subjects' interpretations. Although these indigenous interpretations are always part of the observations that we should account for, they need to pass through the tests of variation and need to show their valence in action. Focusing on neither first-person perspectives nor third-perspective explanations that work behind people's backs, such an approach provides what may be termed a second-person explanation—one that is in serious dialogue with our interlocutors' explanations without necessarily agreeing that their interpretations are the strongest ones available.

Similarly, a pragmatist explanation is not limited to the most immediate observable causes. As long as the researchers are able to extend causality empirically, they can go beyond immediate causes to see how a pattern is shaped either by its history or by larger structural forces. Such a deliberate search for causes behind causes, however, cannot be decided on in advance, but only after the pattern of consequences-in-action has been construed. And, unless the researcher begins a new project to test these causal pathways, such extensions may lose some of the complexity and nuance of data-set variation, as they will usually deal with a smaller universe of phenomena to be explained, with little variation to support the causal line they draw from extension to case.

Finally, although we have treated variation and causality in two different chapters, these aspects of theorization are intertwined. In any qualitative research project, we must examine semiotic sequences and their variations: the patterned set of observations that is used to produce and reject abductive inferences constitutes a phenomenon to be explained. We use consequences-in-action to explain the phenomenon we have focused on and then recursively refine our understanding of how the observations constitute a case. And while defining the contours of variation, we necessarily presume and develop a causal account.

7: THE COMMUNITY OF INQUIRY

One of the ironies of qualitative research is that researchers reveal how the social world shapes other people's lives while carefully hiding how their own social relations craft their theories. We cherish the image of the lone genius returning to a desk after spending arduous hours in the field or archives. And yet the social context of inquiry is central to the work of theory construction and its reception. A careful look at researchers' lives finds other people's fingerprints everywhere. Ideas emerge at presentations of ongoing work at workshops, courses, colloquia, and conferences. Peers and mentors are thanked in a publication's acknowledgments. Anonymous reviewers for journal articles, grants, and books often give invaluable advice.[1] Book reviews, book and paper awards, author-meets-critics sessions at conferences, published debates, and referencing others' work shape the way projects are evaluated after their publication.

One of the most visible examples of the role other people play in research occurs during academic job talk in the United States. A student presents her qualitative research to an academic audience. The stakes are high: she has been working for several years on the project, and the presentation may determine whether she will be employed. She usually only has forty-five minutes to present her work, followed by about forty-five minutes of audience questions. Job-talk audiences are often not completely friendly: some people may have preferences for a different candidate and many may want to test whether her findings meet contemporary research standards. They usually ask probing questions to test methodological mettle and theoretical contributions.

Answering those questions depends on more than how quickly a job candidate can think on her feet. This is important, but usually not as important as students fear (or hope). Answering the questions largely depends on the steps she has been taking throughout the research process. If the young scholar is sufficiently embedded in an academic social world, no query is completely unexpected because others have challenged her with similar questions throughout her research. Others have already pushed her in the direction of alternative explanations and have asked about the relation between theory and data. In response to these admonitions, she has subjected her own research to what science scholar Bruno Latour called "trials of strength."[2]

It is not only that ideas are stronger if they go through such tests. Ideas are produced in a social world. A community of inquiry, as Peirce called it, provides both the conditions for the emergence of theory, and the criteria through which we assess whether we should believe that the relation between theory and observations is warranted.

Peirce laid the groundwork for his notion of the community of inquiry in a discussion of confidence in science. Instead of trying to determine how people arrive at the ultimate truth, Peirce asked how people rid themselves from angst-provoking doubt to attain a state of belief. Doubt, for Peirce, can be read as the realization of our ignorance, a temporary paralysis of action that may lead to further inquiry. Belief, in contrast, is the "calm and satisfactory state which we do not wish to avoid, or to change to a belief in anything else."[3] Belief is our conviction that we have understood a part of the world around us.

Peirce noted that people often stick to beliefs for reasons that have little to do with intellectual integrity. They do so because of ill-founded individual stubbornness and conviction, because authoritative figures impose their beliefs on them, or because elites embrace a priori notions that support their privileged status. None of these approaches, however, is recommended if we want to resolve doubt. Stubborn tenacity often means that we do not engage with the work that has been done before us, and ultimately leaves us isolated and ignorant. Simply imposing beliefs from a position of power leads to "moral terrorism" based on taste. And a priori elite beliefs may produce a sense of comfort until we are, as Peirce put it, "awakened from our pleasing dream by some rough facts."[4]

Against these dogmatic political forms, Peirce proposed that belief be tested, settled, or rejected through the community of inquiry.[5] As Peirce wrote about philosophy:

> We individually cannot reasonably hope to attain the ultimate philosophy which we pursue; we can only seek it, therefore, for the *community* of philosophers. Hence, if disciplined and candid minds carefully examine a theory and refuse to accept it, this ought to create doubts in the mind of the author of the theory.[6]

Whereas other approaches to resolving doubt rely on preconceived notions, participating in communities of inquiry means that we try to attain belief through an ongoing conversation with the ideas of our peers and intellectual predecessors. Such a community of inquiry should be open to everyone and accessible to all who apply the methods of scientific work. A community of inquiry, in Peirce's mind, should not be committed to a particular belief but to inquiry, to critically questioning existing beliefs by subjecting them to experience, including the method of inquiry itself.[7] Scientific methods aim for collective "belief correction."[8]

Although the unmitigatedly democratic dimension of Peirce's community of inquiry remains out of reach,[9] the insight that we continuously attempt to improve our beliefs while engaging with a social world is crucial. Of course, this does not mean that we naively think of the community in the community of inquiry as a congenial effort to reach a consensus; the community is often combative, manipulative, and competitive.[10] Much like a heated conversation, it is made up of people's lively engaging with each other to become a relevant frame of reference.[11] By engaging in these heated debates and exchanges, researchers receive guidance on how to go about inquiring, on methodological and theoretical tools, on the relevance of observations,[12] and on ways of communicating and disseminating research results.

We argue that participating in a community of inquiry helps qualitative researchers to produce and cull abductive insights in three ways. First, communities of inquiry press the question of *fit*: Is the claim backed up by the observations that the researcher presents? Second, they raise the question of *plausibility*: Are there alternative explanations or theories that do a better job of accounting for the analysis? And third, they bring up the question of *relevance*: If the researcher's theorization fits the data and is considered plausible, what are the implications of the theorization for other research projects? While showing how communities of inquiry shape research-in-the-making, fit, plausibility, and relevance also constitute three key criteria for the evaluation of qualitative research. Of course, neither Peirce nor we believe that an emphasis on the community of inquiry leads to a relativist world. Methods and observations, as we show throughout this book, matter. But they matter within a community of inquiry that partly shapes researchers' claims.[13]

Fit: Does the Evidence State What You Claim?

Data analysis rests on abstraction and generalization, on stating that a group of observations is an instance of a broader theoretical set. The fit of a claim refers to the extent to which it follows from the presented evidence and at the same time transcends the immediacy of the observations. An empirical restatement of the data would have a perfect fit but add little analytical purchase. Questioning fit means questioning the evidentiary basis of a theoretical claim.

In the last two chapters, we developed a positive account of fit. A theorization fits data when it is able to account successfully for different forms of variation—including dataset variation, variation over time, and intersituational variation. Constructing datasets and explanations on the basis of these forms of variation involves culling alternative characterizations of the phenomenon of interest. In the process, researchers increase their confidence in a theorization. And yet, if we were left to our own devices, we would be hard pressed to know whether the fit we have found is satisfactory. Research data is very rarely conclusive, and with the addition of enough clauses and subclauses, a theory may be able to absorb almost any observed variation. After all, it is the researcher who decides that the observation is part of the universe of cases covered by the causal explanation. Even the construction of sets in dataset variation is seldom straightforward. The researcher may think that she has constructed an obvious dataset, only to find that audiences disagree.

Fit, then, is not a given. Rather, the researcher needs to convince the community of inquiry that the fit is compelling. Researchers do so in different ways. Often, they simply assert their authority—they have "been there," have talked to the people, or have sat in the archives.[14] Quite a bit of the methods section in any published research makes this "trust me" claim on the basis of the volume of data or the time spent researching: interviewers detail how many people they talked to; ethnographers flash the quantity of field notes they have written; historical researchers point to the different archives they went to. Inured to these tricks of the trade, academic audiences often treat these claims with healthy suspicion. After all, an interviewer who interviewed three hundred people for four hours each probably did not manage to read each interview more than once or twice (if that); an ethnographer can have thousands of pages of bad notes; visiting the archives is nice, but doesn't quite get at the work done in them. Increasingly, when a researcher presents a claim, whether in an article, at a conference, or during a job talk, the audiences want to be able to judge for themselves whether the fit between observation and theorization is compelling.

One way of convincing such audiences is to show them some of the evidence that supports the researchers' conclusion. When researchers present some of their observations, readers have a better vantage point from which to judge whether the inferences are warranted or whether the researchers are simply asking their readers to trust them. Historians Steven Shapin and Simon Schaffer refer to such conventions for conveying credibility as "literary technologies" that allow for virtual witnessing aimed at creating assent in a scientific community: "The technology of virtual witnessing involves the production in a *reader's* mind of such an image of an experimental scene as obviates the necessity for either direct witness or replication."[15] Here the text becomes a visual source that gives the impression of verisimilitude. The aspired form of objectivity combines the researchers' authority with the power of observational data.[16]

In other words, the most important way to establish fit depends upon increased transparency in claims making: a community of inquiry should be able to reconstruct the claims and determine whether the theoretical inferences are indeed based on the observations. The implication is that qualitative writing should open up the material to reanalysis by other members of the community of inquiry. Theories thus become, at least partially, intersubjectively ascertainable: people may agree or disagree about evidentiary relationships between observations and abductive claims.

Of course, a skeptic could point out that qualitative researchers present in their published work a tiny sliver of the massive amounts of collected data. It would follow that trust is still paramount for any qualitative research, and that because researchers put only their best foot forward, the observations presented would obviously fit their theorization. Although we agree that a minimal level of trust is crucial—readers have to believe that the observations the researcher presents stand for other observations that were left on the editing floor—we believe that such a skeptic does not read much qualitative research. Researchers routinely present data that blatantly conflicts with their theorization.

Here is an extreme example from an academic book about death and dying. At the end of a chapter on contemplating death, David Moller wrote:

> Not one dying person has ever told me that he or she wished they had a bigger bank account or had achieved greater financial success. Dying persons place greatest value not on material or financial well-being, but on relief of suffering, social support, spiritual fulfillment, and finding meaning.[17]

Preceding this conclusion, Moller presented a nine-page story of a thirty-four-year-old mother of four who was diagnosed with a brain tumor. He quoted the woman's narrative: The physicians "decided to run a CT scan on my head. I asked them if it was absolutely necessary. I can see the expense now. The baby needs new shoes and I desperately need to take Scott to the dentist." Later, she added,

> I contacted special services this afternoon to see if anything can be done financially. You want to hear something real funny? They say that we make

too much money! I laughed. Be real. They tell me that if indeed I die, they will be able to help the boys. Something must be terribly wrong with this country if we put such little value on a human life. Don't I have more to offer to this world if I live? Can only my death release the resources that are needed? They can't offer much help, red tape and all that stuff, they explain. Perhaps if I sell all my stock, sell my car and reduce my assets to under $2,200 per month I can apply for Medicaid next month.[18]

Finances came up again a couple of days later:

We discussed cost with the office at [the hospital.] They are going to write off half for teaching purposes. Dr. also agreed to reduce his fee. Either way, though, it will financially wipe us out. I've sold our stock. That was so hard too, as it was the only thing that was left me from my grandmother. Next month I will be eligible to receive Medicaid. But that is two weeks away and I can't wait that long for this operation. It's like a Catch 22.[19]

The researcher's claim that no dying person has ever cared about money is contradicted by an example provided only pages earlier: this young mother leaving a family behind worried extensively about the cost of her treatment and depleting her family's financial reserves. The analytical claim in this case seems to follow from a preconceived notion of a "humanitarian death" that romanticizes past dying in community settings and singles out technology as the major culprit for loneliness and alienation at the end of life. It does not fit the data. And yet Moller's extensive quoting allows his readers to double-check his claims and find the discrepancy. Rather than being simply a rhetorical tool, then, presentation of interview material provides readers with an ability to reconstruct the argument from observations.

The search for fit does not emerge only at job talks or when we are reading a finished manuscript. If the researcher is enmeshed in a community of inquiry, questions of fit cull dubious abductive inferences well before they see the light of day. When we teach qualitative research methods, we ask students to present a noticeable field note excerpt and tell us what it is a case of. The discussion is often sobering because it shows the gap between what aspiring researchers hope their data states and the claims actually afforded by the research. In a fascinating study of mental health outreach workers, graduate student Neil Gong chose the following fragment:

I saw the shadow of a person around the corner of the house, and we walked over to say hello. José is a 31 year old man, very skinny, with a dark moustache. He was wearing a baseball hat backwards. He sat down to tie his shoes, which had disproportionately long laces. "What do you want?" he asked us. Deirdre (a mental health nurse) told him that we were just coming to check on him and offer him some help. He said he didn't want any help. Deirdre told him that his mother is worried about him, and he said again he didn't want our help. He then stood up and walked away, around the back-side of the house. Deirdre turned to Chris (a social worker) and asked him to go talk to José, because, "Maybe, you know, the guy thing." Chris walked around the way, but we then saw José hop the fence and start running. Deirdre said, "Oh, he's very scared."

José's mother then explained to us that she's had to call the police, but she doesn't like to, because they send in too many officers. We walked down the street and saw him. Chris said, "Well, as far as he's concerned, we're the mental health cops. And that is kinda what we are right now." When José saw us walking toward him he started running again. We got in the car and I drove, not on purpose, in his same direction. Deirdre saw him and decided to get out of the car, but he ran off again. She later told me that at least he knows we are not the psychiatric mobile response team, because the emergency team would have called the cops when he ran. Chris again mentioned the fact that the county car scares people.

Neil initially interpreted this fragment as an instance of "mental health impression management." The mental health workers, Neil wrote:

attempted to show themselves to be trustworthy to the son, as he thinks the team is there to take him away. This is a case of a institutional role blurring, as the team must attempt to present itself to the son as simply there to help him, not as agents of the police, while simultaneously acting as the guard for the scared mom who has called them as a secondary form of the police.

In class, we projected the data on a white board and then asked the other students to comment on the fragment and on what they thought of Neil's interpretation.

The student discussion focused on the basic question of who was doing what in this instance. Neil's peers pointed out that they did not see the mental health workers either taking pains to establish trustworthiness or acting as guards for José's mom. The only indication of trustworthiness is Deirdre's mention of checking on him and offering help. Instead, the crux of the data shows members of the mental health team explaining to themselves why José started running when they stopped by. They explained his behavior by saying that José presumed that they were part of law enforcement, an explanation prompted by José's mom, who admitted that she had called the police on other occasions.

The class's interpretation shifted the locus of action from a mental health team conveying particular kinds of expressions to outsiders to an internal discussion about how the team is perceived by others. This shift in what the data says matters because it leads to a very different project: from studying impression management to exploring professional justification. Neil agreed that his data supported the internal interpretation. In a later version, he wrote:

> The following passages show how treatment-team members narrate and justify to themselves why clients or potential clients refuse their services. Reasons given include the utter mysteriousness of human behavior, people's real fears of coercive and dangerous situations, and psychopathology.

This second statement retold the observations in slightly more abstract terms.

The exercise points to the two analytical weaknesses with which we began the book: weakly founded theorization and thinly veiled description. Some scholars—including Neil in his initial attempt—hope that data can be extended in ways that did not seem to emerge in the observations. Others, realizing the dangers of unsubstantiated theorization (or just shying away from abstraction) simply summarize the data without an attempt at theoretical abstraction. In the first situation, a theorization seems so compelling that the data are, by and large, ignored. In the latter, description is a safe but analytically unsatisfying route. In the latter case, fit is not much of a question because the researchers do not generalize at all but simply describe— theorization is sacrificed on the altar of fit.

The class presentation is an ideal environment for the production of abductive inferences. Researchers present data and theorizations to others, who then question whether the fit the researcher sees is largely a figment of the imagination, or whether they too can see how observations connect to theorization. Such a discussion can move the researcher in different directions. Neil could have, for example, tried to come up with a different abduction to explain his case. Perhaps, following the discussion, he could focus on processes of blaming third parties for intervention failure, and ask himself whether moving the blame to potential clients, families, and other agencies (such as the police) routinely happens in the field.

The fact that the data excerpt Neil chose did not support his original theorization did not necessarily mean that he should discard his theoretical hunch, as long as he realized that the data did not match the analysis. He could have instead decided that the theoretical instance pointed to a more interesting project than what he had been doing, and he could have revised his data-gathering strategy accordingly. Neil could have surmised that the internal rationalizations reflected the erosion of governmental welfare functions, which led to a blurring of mental health treatment and law enforcement, with the latter picking up the slack of an eroded mental health safety net. As students in class quickly realized, though, the excerpt did not support this provocative hypothetical. Still, Neil produced an intriguing theoretical hunch that could have required him to rethink his research project and focus on the relationship between mental health outreach and law enforcement in a crumbling welfare state. Following this abductive possibility would require additional data gathering specifically around street situations that involve mental health and law enforcement to see how they were resolved, or engagement in a historical study of the role of law enforcement in community mental health. This line of reasoning may be a dead end, or it may reinvent someone else's project — or it may lead to something new and innovative.

Enlisting the community of inquiry in establishing a convincing fit is an important part of buttressing a theoretical statement, as the example of Moller's unfortunate generalization makes clear. Allowing others access to the relationship between data and theory early on is crucial both as a way to avoid future mistakes and to push the researcher in new directions. This form of feedback helps recalibrate the research design so the researcher can pursue abductive hunches, which may require a shift in data gathering if they are not supported by the evidence the researcher has already collected.

Plausibility: What Are the Alternative Explanations?

The community of inquiry's input into the research process goes beyond establishing the fit between abductive inference and data. When people question the fit of a specific abductive possibility, they also are likely to suggest other possible explanations. Even if the inference does seem to fit the observations, there could be alternative theoretical accounts that make equal, if not better, sense to the audiences we speak and write to. Such suggestions question the plausibility of the researcher's theoretical account by providing compelling alternative explanations.

As with the question of fit, questions of plausibility do not come from out of the blue. After all, the search for different forms of variation is meant not only to facilitate inference but also to cull other abductive possibilities. Yet without recourse to the community of inquiry, this task of culling abductive alternatives would be insurmountable. As Peirce noted, an infinite number of alternative abductions exist for any single abductive possibility that the researcher follows. How do researchers know which alternative explanations to reject in order to make their own abductive inference compelling?

An example of how plausibility is questioned and defended can be seen in a sociological debate about social isolation. In the aftermath of the 1995 Chicago heat wave, which claimed 739 lives, Eric Klinenberg[20] produced a study that showed that different neighborhoods had different mortality rates. In one of his most provocative theses, he argued that in order to understand why, for example, seventeen people died in one poor black neighborhood, but only two in an adjacent Latino neighborhood, sociologists must pay attention to structural forces:

> A key reason that African Americans had the highest death rates in the Chicago heat wave is that they are the only group in the city segregated and ghettoized in community areas with high levels of abandoned housing stock, empty lots, depleted commercial infrastructure, population decline, degraded sidewalks, parks, and streets, and impoverished institutions. Violent crime and active streetlevel drug markets, which are facilitated by these ecological conditions, exacerbate the difficulties of using public space and organizing effective support networks in such areas.[21]

The widely read study attracted criticism from a fellow ethnographer, Mitchell Duneier.[22] One of Duneier's key critiques was that the project was theoretically misconceived. Although Klinenberg dealt with specific people's deaths, his unit of analysis was the neighborhood rather than individuals. Thus, Duneier argued, Klinenberg had committed an ecological fallacy—using neighborhood-level ecological data to make claims about individual lives. To back up this claim, Duneier went to Chicago and interviewed some of the families and friends of the deceased in one neighborhood. On the basis of these interviews, he argued that the causes of death were different from those posited by Klinenberg. People who died in South Lawndale mostly lived with other people and thus were not isolated; many of them abused alcohol or drugs.

Whether Klinenberg or Duneier has the upper hand in this debate is beside our point. The structure of the debate warrants our attention because it is an ideal site for the determination of plausibility in qualitative research, as well as an instructive case in which we can see the relationship between plausibility and fit of a research claim.

Duneier's criticism of Klinenberg's book *Heat Wave* proceeded in three stages: he questioned the plausibility of Klinenberg's theorization, then his research design, and finally his findings. The problem wasn't that the data Klinenberg presented didn't fit his theory. They did, and admirably so. Rather, Duneier argued, the research design was based on misleading structural and ecological theoretical assumptions. Because he assumed a neighborhood-level explanation, Klinenberg did not examine some of the individual-level data he could have easily found. If he had done so, he would have found that the data did not fit his theorization after all. Instead of the ecological effects Klinenberg posited, different possibilities would have emerged—that poverty and underemployment in some black neighborhoods meant that people couldn't invest in the purchase or upkeep of air conditioning, or that poverty and underemployment led people to abuse drugs and alcohol, thus making them more vulnerable to extreme weather conditions.

In other words, questioning plausibility leads to a rethinking of research design. This, in turn, leads to the gathering of new data that may or may not fit the proposed theorization. A different chain of consequences-in-action is posited and a different causal explanation offered. In defending his theorization, Klinenberg criticized the reliability of the data Duneier had gathered in Chicago, went on to gather more data on his own, and argued that this new data also fit the theoretical narrative he originally produced.[23] People were in fact isolated; they did not die because they abused drugs or alcohol. Duneier's interviews were highly flawed, relying on reconstructions of the events ten years after the fact.

More generally, this debate shows how, when plausibility is questioned, a different framework refracts the entire project. In most cases plausibility debates do not emerge after the research is published, but while the research is ongoing. Different possibilities are examined in response to questions by others in the community of inquiry, as well as on the researchers' own initiative as they think about how different possibilities and theories would fit the data they have.

One answer to the question of plausibility is to spell out the assumptions and empirical puzzles that a different theoretical framework entails, to show why the abductive possibility chosen is the right one for the specific set of questions the researcher asks about observations, and why other theoretical lenses would not be helpful for answering these particular questions. At the same time, challenges to plausibility such as the one in the *Heat Wave* debate also have a highly creative potential: they force us to spell out taken-for-granted assumptions and may reveal blind spots in our thinking.

The development of a theoretical argument creates what philosopher Alan Garfinkel calls a contrast space, or the relative context in which an answer to a puzzle makes sense. Garfinkel argues that a single general question may lead to various contrast spaces because it rests on different suppositions and has various consequences. Jokes often play with differing contrast spaces: Why do ducks fly south in winter? The answer: Because it is too far to walk. The joke supposes the contrast space that ducks may fly south, west, east, or north in winter; the answer focuses on flying versus walking south. Garfinkel's point is that a successful answer needs to speak to the question at hand and that by specifying a particular question we can limit the realm of possible alternative answers: "Two explanations are inconsistent with each other, or can be conjoined, or are irrelevant to each other, only if their contrast spaces line up in certain ways."[24] A theory establishes a set of equivalence relationships of phenomena bound together by similar propositions. Challenging a research project with a plausible alternative theorization presumes a different kind of contrast space.

The notion of theoretical contrast spaces draws attention to how in abductive analysis researchers gradually tighten links between observations and theorizations over the course of their research. This tightening does not mean that alternatives are inconceivable but that research is geared toward finding an explanation for variation that holds for specific conditions. Posing plausible alternatives may create awareness about the limitations of one's explanation, reveal the specificity of the variation, or point to holes in the explanations and theorization. The constructive result of challenging research with plausible alternatives may lead the researcher to acquire different observations or adapt the theorization.

In qualitative research, both the issue of neglected plausible alternatives and the suspicion that the data fit only because the causal field was manipulated in a way that is hard to justify are not limited to academic disputes. Researchers need to think not only about the often insular-seeming comments, reviews, and scholarly back-and-forth that they expect, but also about alternatives that people in the field and intelligent lay interlocutors can mobilize. As Jack Katz notes about ethnography, "Lay readers do not need access to special procedures or to the specialized language of methodological criticism to raise potentially devastating critiques to an ethnographer's substantive claims."[25] Rather than simply positing research in relation to the state of the field, researchers need to think through some of the alternatives that lay readers may posit. This also allays the danger of making academic work an echo chamber in which theorizations are plausible only because researchers have collectively suspended certain questions that lay readers may raise. A broad, inclusive community of inquiry thus functions as a system of checks and balances on theoretical plausibility.

Relevance: So What?

The "So what?" question signals that defeat can still be snatched from the jaws of victory. This question implies that your audience has no fundamental quibbles with your methodology, research, and theoretical innovations but wonders whether the entire endeavor is worth the effort. Critics may dismiss the project as trivial, obvious, or insignificant; they may want you to spell out why other researchers would want to read your project if they are not particularly interested in the substantive issues. Diane Vaughan's *Challenger* study will be of immediate relevance to audiences interested in the *Challenger* launch disaster and to a handful of scholars interested in spacecraft accidents. In order to reach a broader academic readership, however, her work had to be relevant for other sets of questions and debates. Relevance, like fit and plausibility, is not intrinsic to a study; it is something that researchers need to achieve by broadening the interest of their project in dialogue with a community of inquiry.

The discussion of relevance brings us back to the pragmatic maxim: concepts and theories need to be evaluated for their potential practical effects — their ability to lead to practical commitments or consequences. The pragmatic maxim highlights the critical importance of constructing theories that connect with other people's practices and that make a difference in thinking.

Of course, qualitative research has various warrants: reasons other researchers would be interested in a project.[26] A warrant could simply be that a study lifts the veil off a world readers didn't know. It may be that the researcher sheds new light on old problems by identifying an especially important policy logic or by revealing causes behind causes in an elegant explanation. The research may have a broader substantive scope than previous studies on the same topic, or may challenge our taken-for-granted preconceptions about a group. The work may simply provide a methodological exemplar that inspires other qualitative researchers. Even with little theoretical acumen, researchers can make their work relevant in these ways.

If the theorization the researcher constructs is to be the hook for relevance, the question "What is this a case of?" transforms into an inquiry about whether these cases matter in a broader theoretical debate. As opposed to questions of fit and plausibility, there are no clear methodological guidelines researchers can follow in the search for theoretical relevance. Researchers need to use their imaginations and develop the theoretical generalization they constructed. They need to think about how their theorization will help other researchers, who are studying other cases, to see something new in their data or to organize their research differently. In other words, they have to begin to outline the potential uses of their generalization.

As with fit and plausibility, the community of inquiry works as a double-edged sword in enhancing a project's theoretical relevance: pointing out weaknesses but also offering suggestions for strengthening theoretical ties. In many situations—whether in discussions, comments, or reviews—members of the community of inquiry push researchers to think through the relevance of their work. Their advice may often seem harsh, but it is critical in addressing the "So what?" question. It pulls researchers from being enmeshed in their own case and requires them to think more broadly. At best, such incitements provide researchers with the opportunity to ponder potential uses for their research.

To exemplify the effort necessary to establish theoretical relevance, we outline the work of Robert Jansen,[27] who shared successive drafts of his study of collective memory. Jansen shows how a community of inquiry, in this case editors and reviewers, pushed him to conceptualize the potential implications of his research for other scholars.

Jansen's study began as a comparative historical research project of the uses of historical figures in Mexico and Nicaragua. The puzzle he tried to answer was how historical trajectories in the two countries shaped the way revolutionaries could construct some of their most powerful symbols in collective memory. He realized that in Nicaragua, the Sandinista revolutionaries resurrected the image of a past hero, Augusto Sandino, and this cultural crafting of their hero was accepted, even by their opponents. In Mexico, however, the collective memory of another revolutionary, Emiliano Zapata, seemed more constrained, and even though revolutionaries ended up being able to reinvent him, they needed to actively reappropriate him as a symbol. As he researched the archives, Jansen realized that the key to understanding the difference was to follow the reputational trajectory of each dead revolutionary. In Mexico, the figure of Zapata had been co-opted by the state. Consequently, his reappropriation as a revolutionary figure was fraught with conflict. In Nicaragua, where no such co-optation had occurred, the path was clear for the creation of a revolutionary symbol. Theoretically, Jansen argued that the trajectories of collective memory powerfully shape how "memory entrepreneurs" can act; they influence the challenges and opportunities they face. A collective memory, he argued, does not operate in a vacuum but is shaped by its own historical career.

As Jansen approached journals about publishing his study, his theoretical contribution was questioned. The first journal rejected his article when reviewers argued that his theoretical account was a nice explanation of two specific historical cases, but that except for stating a rather obvious point—that the crafting of a collective memory is historically constrained—his work

POSSIBLE COMBINATIONS OF INHERITED SYMBOLIC CONDITIONS

Combination	Salience	Valence	Ownership	Immediate Implication
1	S	+	P	Advantageous
2	S	+	A	Threatening
3	S	+	0	Neutral
4	S	−	P	Threatening
5	S	−	A	Advantageous
6	S	−	0	Neutral
7	S	0	P	Neutral
8	S	0	A	Threatening
9	S	0	0	Neutral
10	N	NA	NA	Neutral

NOTE.—S = salient; N = not salient. + = positive valence; − = negative valence; 0 = neutral or ambivalent valence. P = protagonist; A = antagonist; 0 = other.

FIGURE 5. Possible permutations of salience, valence, and ownership of the social memory of historical figures. (Robert Jansen, "Resurrection and Appropriation: Reputational Trajectories, Memory Work and the Political Use of Historical Figures," *American Journal of Sociology* 112, no. 4 [2007]: 989).

did not add much to the literature. The reviewers found relatively little to argue about in his analysis. The theorization fit the data and was plausible. Yet the proposition that memory is historically constructed seemed too obvious and thus irrelevant for the scholars who reviewed his work.

Rather than sadly putting the project aside, Jansen reworked his paper. He clarified his data collection procedures, tried to sharpen the analysis of his cases, and sent the article to a different journal. Yet again, the reviewers of his work found that his study was hard to generalize beyond the specific cases he followed. More charitable than the reviewers of the first journal, they allowed him to revise his paper for possible publication. Both the reviewers and the journal's editor warned that publication was contingent on addressing questions of theoretical generalizability. If the reputational trajectories of historical figures mattered, could he show how they would matter beyond the two cases he studied? Jansen decided that rather than simply noting more cases in the article's conclusions as an appeasement strategy, he would explicitly theorize the process through which reputational trajectories matter, and show how the development of the theoretical logic of his work could be generalized.

Jansen hit upon three different axes that mattered in both of his cases — the figure's salience in collective memory (strong or weak); the valence of the figure's reputation in collective memory (positive, negative, or ambivalent); and the ownership of the figure's memory (by the protagonist, the antagonist, or others). By developing the different aspects of reputational trajectories, Jansen developed a theoretical model that was much more general than the empirical materials he had and included many more potential ramifications. Rather than having only two possibilities, he suddenly had ten starting points (see fig. 5), which actors could then attempt to change, resulting in a "mind boggling"[28] number of permutations.

As Jansen showed, a plethora of different trajectories could emerge. Although he exemplified only two of them in his own study, by outlining the contours of the model he could point to possible interpretations of other situations and figures far removed from Mexico and Nicaragua—from Mao's use of the image of Confucius in China, to Khrushchev's recoding of the figure of Stalin from a benevolent father of the Russian nation to a despot, all the way to the American civil rights movement's mobilization of President Lincoln's image. The elaboration of a theoretical model allowed Jansen to move from generalization to potentiality, from theoretically explaining two cases to creating a set of tools usable by others.[29]

As Jansen's example clearly shows, working through the questions of theoretical relevance is not simply an exercise in favorably spinning a research project—adding a few footnotes or an offhand paragraph to placate reviewers. A researcher's first reaction may be to dismiss a critical reader's request that she think beyond the specific theorization that she has spent a long time constructing. A better strategy is to presume that these comments are made in good faith. If the theorization is not relevant to others, the work will not see the light of day or will quickly disappear into off-site library stacks after publication. In order to make a study relevant, a researcher may want to extend the causal field or to link the data to other research projects or broader sociological debates. Most important, as we can see in Jansen's example, the researcher may want to deepen the study's theoretical logic and demonstrate how a case study may be relevant for other projects.

Conversing in a Community of Inquiry

As Peirce argued, science does not discover a singular, timeless, absolute truth. "Science," he wrote, "is not standing upon the bedrock of fact. It is walking upon a bog, and can only say, this ground seems to hold for the present. Here I will stay till it begins to give way."[30] A theoretical claim would withstand doubt if we were to inquire as far as we fruitfully could in the matter, and if it were an ongoing concern for a community of inquirers rather than for an individual researcher.[31] A theorization adds to an ongoing conversation about the world we live in. And as we do in any ongoing conversation, we must answer to interlocutors—whether our contemporaries or the echoes of our predecessors.

The evidentiary and theoretical discussions of research render qualitative research, like any other science, a social accomplishment, both in its process of creation and in its use by other researchers as they craft their work. Plausibility, fit, and relevance are "dependent upon the depth and scope of the transformative interrogation that occurs in any given scientific community."[32] In the process of working with data and theories—whether in classes, in presentations, in feedback on written drafts or in criticism of published work—researchers engage in a conversation in which they have to constantly defend and articulate their research project, sometimes needing to go back to the field, add theoretical tools, or change their research design.

As research is shaped and reshaped by the reactions of peers and readers, a community of inquiry not only strengthens the arguments the researcher develops, but is crucial in pushing theory construction forward. By challenging researchers to provide evidence of fit and plausibility, and by constantly assessing the relevance of researchers' work, the community of inquiry ensures that claims are backed up with data and that they build further on an existing body of scholarship.

What, however, would stop research from becoming an academic echo chamber, in which researchers repeat hackneyed truisms and follow popular and well-trodden paths to appease their audiences? There is no real guarantee that social engagement during research will produce rather than stifle creativity. It is easy to envision a scientific community that harshly censors dissident views, where straying from intellectual fads or dogma leads to ridicule and reprisals. Pragmatists, especially John Dewey, were adamant that scientific inquiry requires democracy and openness of communication. Achieving the transformative potential in a community of inquiry requires that qualified people have an opportunity to criticize, that recipients are responsive to such criticism, and that criticism and not political power prevails. If those conditions are not met (and some would argue that they are at best unevenly met in contemporary social science), we return to one of Peirce's societies, in which belief is settled dogmatically through the moral tyranny of taste.

We have emphasized face-to-face interactions in which researchers expose their work to external criticism, but part of becoming a researcher is to internalize this ongoing dialogue. A researcher sitting in the privacy of an office may anticipate a community of inquiry. As the text must increasingly show how the researcher connects observation to theorization, the researcher needs to ask herself, again and again, "How would other people understand this excerpt?" "Would they be convinced?" The very fact that the researcher asks these questions strengthens the work. They act as yet another powerful way to defamiliarize the text. Whereas the techniques of defamiliarization we outlined in chapter 4 were designed specifically for observations, here the argument as a whole is defamiliarized. And seeing the text through the eyes of a researcher's interlocutor or an academic significant other often means that the researcher must rethink the project. Abductive potential resides in anticipated and actual dialogue with peers.

CONCLUSIONS: ABDUCTIVE ANALYSIS

Induction and deduction have cast their shadows over qualitative research for too long. Although the most avid practitioners of both logics of inquiry admit that their practices have strayed from methodological recommendations, these theories of method have shaped the imaginations and the research designs of generations of students. This book breaks the stalemate by developing a pragmatist theory of meaning and inference in qualitative research—a theory that allows us to generate and take advantage of the moments of surprise within the research process.

Abductive analysis provides answers to a number of problems that qualitative researchers and theorists of method have encountered in trying to account for the relation among observation, method, and theory. By focusing on creative meaning-making, we move beyond the false dichotomy between the context of discovery and the context of justification. Justification and discovery are part of the same research context. Thinking through semiotic chains and their consequences also allows us to approach the questions of explanation, causality, and variation without falling into the problems that these attempts too often entail. And, perhaps most important, we end up with a theory of method that is geared toward the act of theorization on the basis of empirical materials.

At this point, skeptical readers may raise an eyebrow. Is theory really the alpha and the omega of qualitative research? If everyone were busy theorizing, wouldn't the world just be a cacophony of voices that speak past each other rather than creating a sustained agenda? In the way of conclusions, we want to reiterate the critical role of theories in qualitative research. Theorizing is almost inevitable in sustained qualitative research. Not everyone theorizes explicitly, and this is fine; there are alternative warrants for qualitative research. If researchers carefully attend to the generalizations that they construct out of their data, however, most research projects will find a theoretical voice. Theories allow researchers to reach audiences who may not be interested in the substantive issues of their particular research. Before we develop this point, we review the narrative arc of our pragmatist account and what abductive analysis means for the research process.

Abductive Analysis: An Overview

We began this book by arguing that to understand the relation among data, method, and theory, we must go back to the basic building blocks of inference—to the structure of meaning-making. If we accept the pragmatist architecture of meaning, the rest of the book follows.

The picture that the philosophy of Charles S. Peirce provides for identifying such building blocks is one of an ongoing relation among signs, objects, and interpretants. That is, between a signifying element, the things we signify with it, and the effects of the sign-object on an interpreter. In opposition to more static accounts of meaning that focus on the structure of signs, Peirce tried to explain meaning-making as it unfolds and evolves in practice. The interpretant, the effect of signification, is not a passive outcome but a constitutive element of meaning-making. The three aspects of meaning-making are thus distinct yet interdependent. The object is partly constituted by the sign, but can also resist its signification. Although the interpretant is partly defined by the sign-object, it is also shaped by the habits of thought and action that the interpreter brings into the act of meaning-making. This semiotic relation, in turn, is an ongoing activity: the interpretant of one iteration of meaning-making becomes the sign for the next iteration of meaning-making, and so on, potentially ad infinitum.

Unlike a hermeneutic approach that contextualizes actions by placing them within symbolic layers, a pragmatic approach thus locates the meaning of actions in its effects in iterations of meaning-making. These effects, or consequences, may be actions, thoughts, or emotions. Meaning emerges as ongoing semiotic chains of objects, signs, and interpretants. This position is particularly illuminating because it simultaneously stresses the power of observations and of the observer. As the object offers resistance, not just anything goes: interpretations are limited by experience. This is the extent to which qualitative research has a realist dimension—the specificity of an observation in light of other observations matters. At the same time, the interpretant depends on the habits of thought and action that the researcher has cultivated, and interpreters with different backgrounds and training will pick up and develop different aspects.

This semiotic account is complemented by Peirce's theory of inference. Rather than limiting himself to an analysis of induction and deduction—to inference based on firmed-up hypothesis or to the collection of data—Peirce realized that the structure of inference through which new insights are crafted is different, and he termed this mode of inference abduction. Induction and deduction, as he saw, cannot provide new insights. When we face a surprising fact, we try to puzzle out what would need to have been the case for the surprising observation to make sense or, as he put it, to be "a matter of course." Abduction is this speculative process of fitting unexpected or unusual findings into an interpretive framework.

When we follow Peirce's theory of meaning-making and inference, the tasks and dilemmas of qualitative research become more tangible. Like any other actor in this world, researchers are interpreters and producers of meaning. And like any actor, they routinely perform abductions in their everyday lives as they come across observations they can't immediately make sense of. But there are also important differences between lay actors and researchers. One is that in research we actively look for surprises in the field. Researchers design research to cultivate opportunities for abduction. Another difference is that research constitutes a specific take on the semiotic process: researchers deliberately manipulate the process of meaning-making to typify and explain patterns of observations. This systematic process of meaning-making aimed at theoretical generalizations is what we have termed abductive analysis.

By paying explicit attention to our habits of thought and action, the resistance of objects, and the recursive nature of semiotic chains, we can craft research that aims at abduction. The cultivation of these aspects of meaning-making is the aim of each chapter of this book. Thus, as we argued, to facilitate abduction we need to find ourselves in situations in which we are puzzled by our observations. Fostering empirical surprises is one of the places in which methodology plays a crucial role. First, through meticulous note taking, memo writing, and transcription, we defamiliarize the observations. Like saying a word over and over until it loses its sense, we use these contrivances to distance ourselves from our data. When we do so, the automatic ways we make sense of the world become more fragile, and we find ourselves able to see problems where none seemed to have existed while we were in the field.

In order to leverage methodology for theory construction, we also have to consciously rework our habits of thought and action. Being surprised is important, but if it only results in an all-too-predictable solution or in mild puzzlement, the surprise is wasted on us. Although we come into a field with proto-theories and theories of the social, we never come with just a single theory. Instead, theoretical pluralism needs to be nurtured. If we explicitly foster our ability to look at our data from different theoretical vantage points, we can productively revisit the same defamiliarized phenomenon, looking at it through different theoretical lenses. Thus, the complementary heuristics of defamiliarization and revisiting manipulate both our habits of thought and action and the potential resistance of the objects of our study—increasing the chances that we will find puzzles, and that we can take the same observation and encase it in alternative ways en route to a plausible abduction.

Theory's encasing of an observation, in turn, allows us to move from a single observation to a set. When we form abductions, we implicitly define an observation in relation to things that would be like it; we make an implicit generalization. We understand the observation differently and expect different things of the field, depending on which casing we craft. Moving from a single observation to an explicit set is one of the most important moves that separate everyday meaning-making from research. We do this by systematically comparing observations to each other. Whether we look at dataset variation, variation over time, or intersituational variation, we construct the meaning of what we are studying by casting it as a case of something. When fitting different observations into a category, we often find that the study is not a case of that something after all. Variation thus both provides us with a sense of what kind of case we have—the meaning of the case—and acts as a methodological tool through which we can cull abductive inferences in the act of research.

Whereas forms of variation allow us to construct the meaning of observations across instances and over time and situations, qualitative research also gives us leverage to explain observations—that is, to account not only for what our object of analysis is, but also for why it appears as it does. The move from definition of meaning to explanation of action brings us full circle to the semiotic framework we began with.

Asking about explanations in a pragmatist key is asking about chains of consequences-in-action. Meaning is always constructed on the basis of earlier iterations of meaning-making, and the emerging picture presumes causal sequences. We argue that Peirce's semiotics provides researchers with irreducible building blocks from which they can construct mechanism-based accounts of causality—a continuous and intelligible process that allows us to trace patterns of meaning-making as they emerge in action. Following such consequences-in-action, in turn, allows us to construct an explanatory framework that often goes beyond alternative explanations and the interpretations of actors, as well as providing us with analytic openings to extend our explanation beyond the temporal and spatial framework we began with.

Finally, this relationship among data, theory, and method is mediated by researchers' communities of inquiry, which constitute a simultaneously disciplining and enabling context in which research is assessed according to the evaluative criteria of fit, plausibility, and relevance. In a negative register, our work is always judged, prodded, and poked at by other academics. As we expect these challenges, we defensively double-check the fit of our observations and theory, we worry about whether alternative explanations are plausible, and we consider how to extend our work to reach broader audiences. In a less agonistic mode, communities of inquiry also provide us with insights and with possible avenues of thought. They stimulate us to rethink our categories, the sets we have constructed, and the structure of our explanations. Research and theory construction are part of an ongoing conversation in which both scholars and research subjects take part, challenging our theorizations and suggesting new ones.

What does abductive analysis look like in a research project? Although this book includes quite a few directives—on the level of data organization, the construction of variation, and the tracing of consequences-in-action in the construction of causal accounts—there are a few overarching considerations that structure research. Combining methodological expertise with an in-depth grounding of theories means that qualitative researchers must simultaneously engage in four intertwined activities: they must gather observations, read a broad range of theories, work systematically with their observations, and actively participate in a community of inquiry.

At the early research design stage, researchers must read widely enough to justify spending years on a research topic. They also need to craft a methodologically sound research strategy that anticipates a variety of alternative explanations for a subject area. The goal is threefold. We convince ourselves and our peers that the project has intellectual merit, that it is feasible, and that it has the potential to contribute to or even jump-start conversations within our community of inquiry. Practically, this strategy prepares researchers to recognize surprises in their empirical work; surprises do not simply emerge, but are dependent on deep familiarity with theories. Such an approach to research design may involve a comparative agenda, but in most cases we suggest that the researcher leave the comparison to a later stage. Committing to comparisons at the outset may foreclose interesting additional research questions and sites that come up during the research process.

Once data gathering starts, the researchers begin working on all fronts. They should begin to analyze their data as soon as they conduct their first interviews, read their first batch of documents, or engage in their first observations. They can do so by starting to code their empirical materials in light of their literature reading. This may send them into new literatures or provide them with marching orders for gathering additional materials. Coding for variation leads to writing memos summarizing theoretical inklings and emerging conceptualizations. The questions leading these memos should then be, Do surprises emerge? If so, where? The point of such theoretical memos is to spell out the contexts in which an observation cannot be easily answered by extant theorizations. If a given theorization solves the abductive moment, then our work—at least with regard to the specific observation—is done. But in many cases, digging into the literature exposes deeper misfits and contradictions.

Theoretical memos are a first step in the constitution of the object of our analysis. The next step—analytically, if not temporally—is to move from the specific observation to the constitution of a set. A researcher conducting a project from a pragmatist perspective can trust that the combination of in-depth reading of literatures, immersion in fieldwork, and coding and memo writing will generate anomalous findings that require theoretical alignment. Looking for variation between similar instances, variation of observations over time, and variation of one aspect of the phenomenon in different settings further fosters such anomalies. Examining variation creates a database of data instances to be mined for patterns, processes, and similarities and differences.

Researchers can aim for variation at the start of a research project by taking advantage of the longitudinal and multisited dimensions of the project, but it is often more compelling to decide on the scope of the study as it proceeds. Rather than determining a priori where variation will be most critical, it is often more fruitful to start at one site that we see as promising and then decide during data collection whether our theoretical claims would be strengthened with additional research sites. Comparisons should serve emergent theoretical puzzle solving and not the other way around. As researchers reshape their sets, they continue to rework the object of their analysis: variation not only helps us evaluate abductive inferences but actively shapes them. Throughout this process, researchers try out their abductions with friends, peers, and whoever else will listen to them.

Writing up this research builds further on the memos, theoretical pieces, examined variation, and striking observations the researcher has recorded. In abductive analysis, the key stumbling block for much qualitative research—determining how to frame an argument—becomes the goal of the entire analytic strategy. Still, the skeptic may persist: Should theory be the privileged goal of qualitative research? Don't theoretical generalizations negate qualitative research's unique ability to get close to people's lives?

The Theorist's Predicament

Franz Steiner, an Oxford-trained anthropologist, once lamented the state of theory in his field. Instead of developing theories based on large comparisons, he observed, British anthropologists were going to their fields, usually studying a small portion of a small society, then audaciously generalizing a theoretical statement from their experiences. Dismissing their attempts, Steiner noted that obviously such anthropologists would seem to find something new in the field—theory is general and the field is specific. In the juxtaposition of the general and the specific, something new is bound to emerge.[1] However, he argued, finding new empirical material does not count as proper theory making.

Steiner's diagnosis was exactly wrong in his evaluation of the theorist's predicament. We do, indeed, base our theorizations on the empirical problems we face in a specific field. And, as Steiner argues, it is not a mystery that the juxtaposition of the general and the concrete allows us to find something new and hitherto unnoticed. It is also true that if, at the end of our research project, all we had to say is that our case is a little different, we would be in a sad place indeed. Steiner would be vindicated in his critique. However, that is not all we have to say. When we theorize out of data we say much more.

Where we sharply diverge from Steiner, then, is in his ideal of theorizing. For Steiner, as for many others since, theory making resides in extension: in order to theorize, the theorist surveys the landscape, extending a generalization across disparate fields. Some theorizations are indeed the product of armchair theorists carefully reading a mountain of studies done by others. This is a perfectly respectable form of theorizing. It is, however, only one possibility, and not the most generative one. The difference between the approach we outline here and the kind of theories that Steiner liked so much (and that many students idealize as true theory) is in the way potentiality is produced out of generalization.

Many of the best and most generative theories are based precisely on a deep engagement with an empirical problem encountered in the field. This is true of the theories crafted by Marx and Weber and by Goffman, Geertz, and Bourdieu—whether the engagement occurred in Bali or the British Library, in the Scottish isles or the Berber countryside in Algeria. The reason for this is not incidental: it is precisely by delving deep into their materials that these theorists came to see why previous ways of thinking about their field were partial or were flat-out wrong, and then were able to craft new ways of thinking that fit their observations.

Instead of opting for extension, this form of theorizing emerges from an intensive study of a case. By carefully tracing forms of variation within the case and the chains of consequences-in-action, we are potentially able to locate junctures that are empirically surprising—where abductive inference is required. Sometimes generalizations formed by other researchers can account for these surprising challenges. When they don't, it is not only because our little case has its own little quirk. Rather, it is because something about the logic of the explanation, the generalization's potential to explain new cases, does not work. By delving deeper into the logic of our own explanation—that is, into the general argument hidden in the specifics of our case—we can potentially extend our reach. Rather than starting from extension, we begin by moving inward.

Theorizing is joining a conversation. In conversations, there is not much sense in stopping the exchange, summarizing everything that has been said so far, and then singing the same tune in unison. Of course, when we present our generalizations and potential uses of our case, we need to attend to the ways in which others have generalized their cases. In this sense, our encounter with theory is an encounter with both observations, and with previous theorists' potential avenues for thinking. And yet, much as in a conversation, though others' utterances may be brilliant, they are never final. If, after we have thought of other modes of explanation, we still think that there is something about the structure of our explanation that is not captured by other theories, and if our explanation would change the way others see their own work, then our theory is generative—not despite its limited empirical scope, but precisely because it is based on intensive qualitative inquiry.

Our skeptical reader in the beginning of the chapter wondered why we focus so much on theory. Our answer is simple: if we truly delve into the specifics of our case and take the community of inquiry we are enmeshed in seriously, then theorizing is not a separate form of research. Theory is part of the research act that emerges as we build and problematize the generalizations produced by others and offer generalizations of our own. Much of qualitative research today either produces relatively descriptive accounts or follows a predetermined theoretical approach. The problem of theory currently is not that there is too much of it, but that it is considered a distinct subfield, and something that only established scholars play with.[2] This, we think, is unfortunate. Theory should not replace or be replaced by empirical research; it is part of the same act.

Peirce considered abduction an irreducible, constitutive part of everyday life. People's ability to move fluently between situations, redefine unfolding actions, and transfigure everyday scenes and dramas suggests a kind of situated creativity,[3] a string of abductive moments. Although not all our actions are creative, and we quite often respond routinely to familiar situations, there are always situations that require creative abduction. This view of meaning-making and everyday creativity gives qualitative research both its subject matter and an account of the researcher's work. Theorizing is not the end, but part of a process of intellectual dialogue. It is an ongoing exercise in puzzling out the world we live in, of striving for a final analysis but never completely capturing it.

ACKNOWLEDGMENTS

Abductive Analysis: Theorizing Qualitative Research is the outcome of conversations and exchanges within a large community of inquiry. Acknowledgments only skim the surface.

Several circumstances prompted us to write this book. When teaching qualitative research methods to graduate students, Stefan, and later Iddo, felt that although they were incorporating some working methods from grounded theory, they had to file off the sharp edges of the approach to make it pedagogically workable. Coding and memo writing were well and good, but the whole did not add up to theoretical innovation. Then a maddening experience Stefan had as a reviewer for an National Science Foundation dissertation panel, in which all inductive proposals were summarily nixed because they supposedly signified theoretical ignorance, made writing a book that does justice to the relation among theories, observations, and qualitative methods seem urgent. More positively, this book comes out of the deep passions about methodological integrity we found among our interlocutors in academia and the field, and our own desire to account for the joy of puzzling out evidence theoretically.

Kathy Charmaz asked us to contribute to the *Handbook of Grounded Theory* with a chapter discussing grounded theory and ethnography. Not only did the assignment help us to articulate both the merits of grounded theory and our dissatisfactions with it, but several other chapters in the handbook introduced us to the notion of abduction (thanks Karen Locke, Jo Reichertz, and Jörg Strübing). Intrigued, we started reading Peirce. When we sent out our first article in which we engaged Peirce's thinking, editor and fellow pragmatist Neil Gross provided critical feedback on our understanding of pragmatism, and reviewers encouraged us to claim a name for our approach. A conference at the University of Chicago on causality and ethnographic evidence further helped us to articulate the focus on variation and explanation in chapters 5 and 6. Over the course of many Skype calls between New York and Los Angeles, the ideas in the book gradually took shape. Although one of us may have started a particular chapter or thought, we both rewrote the chapters countless times, so in the end, personal idiosyncrasies have been washed out.

As with all books, we have benefited from both imagined conversations and actual engagements with other researchers. We are indebted to comments from the two readers for the press, one who identified herself, Sharon Kaufmann, and one who remains anonymous. We thank Rene Almeling, Mathieu Berger, Richard Bernstein, Adele Clarke, Jean De Munck, Jacob Foster, Neil Gong, Neil Gross, Robert Jansen, Colin Jerolmack, Nahoko Kameo, Jack Katz, Sarah Morando, John O'Brien, Laura Orrico, Sara Shostak, Forrest Stuart, Diane Vaughan, and Ann Swidler for extended conversations and for comments on parts or all of the manuscript. We also thank Tim McGovern and Doug Mitchell of the University of Chicago Press for making the publication of this book such a pleasure. We would like to single out Doug Mitchell for his enthusiastic support for the book. Finding a fan of Peirce in an editor was more than we could plausibly have hoped for.

The last paragraph of an acknowledgment section is typically a shout out to family members. Unlike some of Stefan's other books, this book required few family sacrifices. Still, Ruth's good-natured encouragement and Merel and Jasper's inquisitive queries helped move this project along. Iddo would like to thank Nahoko for long conversations into the night, as well as for suffering through the Skype interferences in their lives, and he thanks Eliana for making him realize how full of surprises everyday life can be.

APPENDIX: A SYNOPSIS OF ABDUCTIVE ANALYSIS

Grant proposals and papers often require a short summary of methodology for audiences with little familiarity with the methodology or patience for a long and subtle exposition. Here is a general way of summarizing abductive analysis as a method of analysis. You may adapt this to the specific characteristics of your project:

We analyzed the data in this study using the principles of abductive analysis. Abductive analysis is a qualitative data analysis approach grounded in pragmatism and aimed at theory construction. Abduction refers to the process of producing theoretical hunches for unexpected research findings and then developing these speculative theories with a systematic analysis of variation across a study. This approach depends on iterative processes of working with empirical materials in relationship with a broad and diverse social science theoretical literature.

We sought out surprising findings in light of what would have been expected on the basis of the literature [specify literature]. This search for unexpected findings was facilitated by note taking, memo writing, transcription, and coding of the empirical materials [specify]. Through this analytical process we determined that a critical ongoing concern of the study was the following phenomenon of interest [specify]. Once we defined this phenomenon of interest, we systematically examined the variation of this phenomenon among the accumulated data. Specifically, we explored how the phenomenon of interest varied across the data, over time, and across situations, at each point redefining the characteristics of the phenomenon of interest in light of similarities and differences. We then traced the processes through which such variation emerged; this provided us with a mechanism-based explanation of why the phenomenon of interest occurred.

Abductive analysis can be evaluated with three criteria: fit (Are the theoretical claims supported by the empirical materials?), plausibility (Are the theoretical claims stronger than competing theories?), and relevance (Do the theorizations matter in the broader intellectual community?). To establish the fit of our theoretical claims, we examined variation and looked for negative cases that would require an adjustment to the theory. We enhanced plausibility by comparing our theory with the following theories [specify and discuss the strength and weaknesses of each theory]. The relevance of this study is apparent in the following contributions to scholarship [specify].

NOTES

Introduction

1. Geertz (1973).
2. Hammersley (1992).
3. Abbott (2004); Becker (1998).
4. Hammersley and Atkinson (1983).
5. Glaser (1992b).
6. See National Science Foundation's reports on qualitative methods: Ragin, Nagel, and White (2004); Lamont and White (2005). See also Culyba, Heimer, and Petty (2004).
7. Denzin and Lincoln (1994).
8. Loïc Wacquant (2002) took aim at Mitch Duneier's *Sidewalk* (1999), Katherine Newman's *No Shame in My Game* (1999), and Elijah Anderson's *Code of the Street* (1999). Mitch Duneier (2004; 2006) then targeted Eric Klinenberg's *Heat Wave* (2002). A squadron of ethnographers took issue with Wacquant's *Body and Soul* (2004); see the 2005 special issue of *Qualitative Sociology* 28 (2) and the review essays in *Symbolic Interaction* 28 (3), also published in 2005. Cultural anthropology saw an intriguing debate between Marshall Sahlins (1981, 1995) and Gananath Obyesekere (1992) that revolved around the imputation of different forms of rationality to "natives" and was waged through the question of the relation between data and theory in the analysis of the deification and death and Captain Cook in Hawaii.
9. Note that the extended case method is not actually deductive. Inspired by the work of philosopher Imre Lakatos (1976), practitioners of the extended case method seek to amend predefined theorizations rather than simply use them to make sense of data. However, as we discuss in the next chapter, predefining the theoretical trajectory of a body of research is largely a deductive move, and one that has serious repercussions in research design, so that the products of research are often uncomfortably deductive.
10. Indeed, these pitfalls lead some qualitative researchers to simply ignore theories of method. Although many great research projects thus sidestep the question and instead merely refer to some of the theories they use—whether Foucauldian theory, pragmatist philosophy, actor-network theory, or other approaches—we believe that sidestepping the theory of method both allows such researchers to

cut corners in their research and impoverishes the collective effort to forge a lively community of inquiry.

11. Our aim is thus not to provide a philosophical exegesis but to appropriate some key pragmatist tenets to help jump-start qualitative data analysis. It is not our objective to provide a synopsis of Peirce's thinking. The works of Bernstein, Gallie, Liszka, Misak, Short, and other Peirce scholars provide a much more comprehensive introduction to Peirce's thought. We have, rather, selectively used some insights we have found in his work as they have proved illuminating for the problems at hand.

12. This remains a point of contention in grounded-theory circles. See the next chapter for more detail.

13. Popper (1959). Until recently, sociologists had little to say about the relation between discovery and justification. Merton wrote a short and brilliant piece on serendipity in which, not incidentally, he cites Peirce in a footnote; Merton and Barber (2006). See also Swedberg (2012).

14. There are, of course, other notions of theorization. We can imagine theory, for example, as the exegesis of other people's texts, which intellectuals interpret and compare in the privacy of their offices, or as the construction of epochal theories seemingly unencumbered by research but with some selected illustrations. See Abend (2008). While we do not want to stake out a single correct form of theorizing, we note that such forms of theorizing are not beholden to research in the same way. Because we believe that observations have a tendency to be far more interesting than anything we can imagine about them beforehand, we opt for a form of theorizing that is observation-based.

15. Winship (2006).

Chapter 1

1. The publisher SAGE alone has more than fifty books on this topic, and researchers have a large choice of data analysis programs. The glaring misconception about these programs is that they conduct the analysis for the researcher. They do not. These programs should be thought of as interfaces between data and various data organization functions such as coding and memo writing. The programs may offer functions for attaching codes to pieces of text or for mapping the codes in a diagram with bubbles and arrows, but they do not tell you what codes to attach to the data. They do not by themselves lead to good or sufficient data analysis. In fact, programs can give students and research groups such a misleading sense of accomplishment: instead of coding to abstract data on a theoretical level, software users may simply summarize the data. They produce many codes in a short amount of time, but the codes are of little analytical value. There are no short cuts in research: you have to conduct the analysis, and it depends on people rather than on bits and bytes. Using a software program to aid qualitative data analysis is very different from using one for quantitative data analysis. Doing a regression analysis via computer rather than by hand makes a tremendous difference

in time, accuracy, and statistical analysis possibilities. There is no equivalent in qualitative research. Researchers should use these programs if they have copious amounts of data; if they would like to combine audio, visual, and text data in the same interface; or if they work with a large research team. But they shouldn't expect the program to produce an analysis.

2. According to Google Scholar (accessed April 16, 2013), *The Discovery of Grounded Theory* in all its translations and misspellings has been cited more than 51,000 times. Weber's *Protestant Ethic* has been cited about 15,000 times. Marx's *Capital* has been cited about 17,000 times. Durkheim's *The Division of Labor* and *The Elementary Forms of the Religious Life* have been cited about 10,000 times each. Granovetter's article on the strength of weak ties is the most cited article published in the *American Journal of Sociology*, with over 23,000 citations. DiMaggio and Powell's article "The Iron Cage Revisited," published in *American Sociological Review*, has been cited more than 21,000 times. We note, however, that although it is often cited, *The Discovery of Grounded Theory* is also quite often used as a placeholder. As with other frequently cited works, citation does not equal engagement.

3. MacMillan and Koenig (2004).

4. Abbott (1997a).

5. Faunce and Fulton (1958).

6. Beauvoir (1965); Sudnow (1967); Tolstoy (1960).

7. Glaser and Strauss (1965).

8. Kübler-Ross (1969).

9. *Awareness of Dying* (Glaser and Strauss 1965), *Time for Dying* (Glaser and Strauss 1968), and the case study *Anguish* (Strauss and Glaser 1970).

10. Glaser (1992b).

11. Bryant and Charmaz (2007).

12. Berger and Luckmann (1966); Blumer (1954); Garfinkel (1967); Kuhn (1962).

13. Strauss (1987).

14. Strauss and Corbin (1990).

15. Coffey, Holbrook, and Atkinson (1996); Dey (1999).

16. Glaser (1992b, 4).

17. Charmaz (2006).

18. Clarke (2005).

19. For a genealogy, see Morse (2009, 17).

20. Charmaz (2000); Hood (2007); Titscher et al. (2000). This diversity of grounded theory approaches is reflected in the capstone *Handbook of Grounded Theory*, where different authors aim to reposition the approach in a changed epistemological force field. One of the major points of contention is the extent to which grounded theory is inductive. Traditionalist grounded theorists hewing closely to Glaser's position maintain that researchers should approach data analysis without theoretical preconceptions, while contemporary grounded theorists who highlight the historical context in which induction was proposed as an alternative to deductive reasoning argue for a deeper engagement with theories. As solutions for the emphasis on inductive reasoning, some grounded theorists have urged a

form of theoretical agnosticism rather than ignorance or have proposed theoretical sampling as a way to broaden the theoretical scope of grounded theory. In our opinion, such repositionings are too tepid: the entire framework of the conceptualization of the relation among theory, observation, and method needs to change, not simply be tinkered with. See also Timmermans and Tavory (2007).

21. Glaser and Strauss (1967, 37).
22. Ibid., 115.
23. Ibid., 91.
24. Ibid., 49; italics added.
25. Ibid., 97.
26. Glaser and Strauss (1967, all quotes p. 46).
27. CP 2.750. Following the conventional referencing style of Peirce scholars, CP refers to Charles S. Peirce's collected writings (Hartshorne, Weiss, and Burks 1931–58). The first number refers to the volume number, and the number after the period refers to the page.
28. Bacon ([1620] 1994).
29. Chalmers (1999).
30. E.g., Collins (1985); Galison (1987); Kuhn (1962); Lakatos (1978).
31. Fine (1995); Glaser and Strauss (1965); Strauss and Glaser (1970).
32. Such as Becker, in Becker, Geer, Hughes, and Strauss (1961); Davis (1963); Goffman (1961); Roth (1963); and Sudnow (1967).
33. Strauss (1993).
34. Clarke (2009); Star (1989).
35. Strauss (1987); Strauss and Corbin (1990).
36. Charmaz (2006); Clarke (2005).
37. Glaser (1992a, 2002).
38. Glaser later abandoned the search for a basic social process; see Glaser (2001).
39. Glaser (1978).
40. Kelle (2007, 200).
41. Strauss and Corbin (1990).
42. Clarke (2005).
43. Charmaz (2009); Clarke (2009).
44. Strauss mentioned Peirce's writings on abduction to emphasize the role of experience in the first phase of research (Strauss 1987, 12).
45. Gluckman ([1961] 2006). The method is also known as situational analysis; van Velsen (1967).
46. van Velsen (1967).
47. Mitchell (1956).
48. Burawoy (1991, 1998, 2000).
49. Burawoy (1998, 5).
50. Burawoy (1998, 16); italics added.
51. See Tavory and Timmermans (2009).
52. Burawoy (1998, 15).

Chapter 2

1. This detour makes sense from a pragmatist perspective. Peirce considered his general theory of signs or semiotics central to his intellectual oeuvre. Especially in his later years, Peirce increasingly linked semiotics to scientific inquiry because inquiry implies a movement from doubt to an understanding of a subject and can thus be understood semiotically (Short 2007). For the relationship between semiotics and pragmatism, see also Morris (1946).
2. Saussure ([1916] 1986).
3. CP 8.343.
4. Peirce scholars disagree regarding his division of the interpretant. Peirce's most famous division is among immediate, dynamic, and final interpretants. Because he used a plethora of terms and changed them abruptly throughout his career, another division he used, between emotional, energetic, and logical interpretants, is sometimes treated as another way of speaking about the same set of distinctions (Liszka 1996; but see also Short 2007).
5. The interpretant is also not necessarily some other person interpreting the act. Peirce had an expansive view of semiotics: animals could act on signs—think of a chameleon changing colors or a dog barking because of a noise—and even machines, such as a motion detector, could be an interpretant of signs in this sense. Because we are primarily interested in social scientists interpreting observations, we limit our discussion to human interpreters.
6. Houser (1998, xxxvi).
7. In its most minimalist sense, his semiotics sets the scene for the symbolic interactionist point that meaning-making is inherently processual. It depends on the actions of specific actors and on how these acts are taken up. Meaning is never automatic, interactionists claim; it is always in motion. The interactionist point, however, lacks the specificity that Peirce puts into his semiotics. Interactionism, based on pragmatism as it was, also failed to take into account the complexities of meaning-making in action. For Herbert Blumer (1969), who coined the term "symbolic interactionism," meaning-making in interaction was always an explicit and reflexive process; for Peirce, on the other hand, meaning-making was often embodied and habitual, not necessarily about cognitive interpretation.
8. For example, Garfinkel (1967).
9. Peirce is well known for his definitions of different forms of signs. Throughout his career, Peirce attempted different kinds of threefold distinctions to capture how different signs operate—the most widely known being his partition of signs into icons, indexes, and symbols (see, for example, Liszka 1996), and others, including the tripartite distinction between Qualisign, Sinsign, and Legisign, and the perhaps better forgotten distinction between rheme, dicent, and delome. The basic logic of division, in each case, is the differentiation between signs that are connected to either object or interpretant in terms of inherent similarities (for instance, color), existential qualities (for example, smoke and fire), or social conventions. For the purposes of this book, however, we are more interested in

Peirce's ideas about inference and about how meaning-making-in-action takes place. See again Liszka (1996) and Short (2007).

10. This aspect of movement from potentiality to generalization (or habitual action) is one that Peirce spent much of his career theorizing. Peirce liked to talk about these aspects of action as firstness, secondness, and thirdness; see, for example, Gallie (1952). However, as with the divisions above, we see little advantage in adding terminological complexity and have refrained from using the Peircian jargon in this instance. Likewise, in the analysis of the interpretant below, we focus on an aspect of what Peirce called the *dynamic interpretant*. Although Peirce distinguished between immediate, dynamic, and final interpretants (as well as between emotional, energetic, and logical interpretants), we decided, for the sake of parsimony, to narrow the scope of our exegesis of Peirce. For excellent, though contending, explications of Peirce's complex divisions of the interpretant, see Liszka (1996) and Short (2007).

11. Peirce scholars mostly agree that when Peirce wrote that the sign determines the object, the relationship should be viewed as one of shaping and limiting rather than a stricter determinism. See, for example, Short (2007).

12. Gibson (1979).

13. Caplow (1984).

14. Tavory and Swidler (2009).

15. Reed (2011)

16. This fits Peirce's distinction between an immediate and dynamic object, in which an immediate object is the object as signified by the sign, and the dynamic object is the object as it goes beyond this initial signification, when we have conducted a "full" inquiry.

17. Sellars ([1956] 1997).

18. Peirce scholars debate over whether his philosophy is best described as realist. We take the stance that although Peirce subscribes to a realist position, this realism is tempered by his understanding of the interpretant; see Misak (1991).

19. Mills (1940).

20. See Silver (2011).

21. See Joas (1996).

22. Davis (1961).

23. Ibid., 121.

24. Ibid., 123.

25. Ibid., 124.

26. Ibid., 128.

27. Ibid.

28. Ibid.

Chapter 3

1. Popper (1959, 31). See also Braithwaite (1953); Reichenbach (1938). For a recent treatment of this distinction, which draws on Peirce and highlights the role of dis-

covery, see Swedberg (2012). Swedberg, however, distinguishes between the contexts of discovery and justification, which, in our view, obstructs his otherwise important analysis. This chapter generally draws from Timmermans and Tavory (2012).

2. Kordig (1978, 110).
3. See, for example, the work of Imre Lakatos (1970, 1976) and Thomas Kuhn (1962).
4. CP 5.171.
5. Although Peirce's understanding of abduction evolved throughout his career and was not always clearly formulated, scholars have distinguished a core set of ideas that present abduction as an inferential process involved in the production of hypotheses (Fann 1970; McKaughan 2008).
6. CP 5.117.
7. For a pragmatist account of causality, see chapter 6.
8. Peirce ([1903] 1997, 282–83).
9. James ([1907] 1981, 95).
10. CP 7.217–18.
11. CP 5.181; italics in original.
12. See also Martin (2011).
13. See, for example, Anderson (2005); Fann (1970); Locke, Golden-Biddle, and Feldman (2008); Paavola (2005); Rescher (1978).
14. CP 5.172.
15. CP 5.173.
16. CP 5.591.
17. CP 5.591; see also Ayim (1974).
18. Thus, for example, critical realism has adopted Peirce's notion of abduction in order to explain how one moves from the realm of the perceived phenomena to what critical realists call the realms of "the actual" and "the real"; see, for example, Bhaskar (1997, 1998). However, without elucidating the sources of abduction, critical realism obfuscates the process of research and uses pragmatist terms as a deus ex machina for what we see as erroneous ontological and epistemological conclusions—abduction does not go deeper into the realm of the real. In a pragmatist account there are no ontological layers such as critical realists wish to introduce.
19. CP 5.181. Using a different philosophical vocabulary, this is what social theorist Alfred Schutz (1967), following Edmund Husserl (1960), would later call apperceptions and appresentations—socialized ways of perceiving the world.
20. James's notion of habit is best captured by his section on the topic in his *Principles of Psychology* (James 1890). The notion of the ready to hand is borrowed from Heidegger ([1927] 1996). See also Dreyfus (1991).
21. See Atkinson (1990); Bourdieu and Wacquant (1992); Burawoy (1998); Macbeth (2001); and Marcus and Fischer (1986) for a discussion of positionality in anthropology and sociology. The examination of the qualitative researcher's role in theorizing the world resembles earlier methodological approaches exhorting researchers to be cognizant of reactivity and research roles (Adler and Adler 1987;

Becker 1967; Hammersley and Atkinson 1983). Qualitative research traditions as diverse as autoethnography, standpoint feminism, interpretive interactionism, reflexive ethnography, and critical race theory put positionality at the heart of methodology; see, respectively, the work of Ellis (1995); Smith (2005); Denzin (2001); Burawoy (2003); and Collins (1992).

22. Robertson (2002, 790).
23. For an account of the role of intellectual biographies in shaping habits of thought, see Brubaker (1993); Gross (2009b). For other discussions of the dangers of simplistic positionality, see Brewer (2000); Murphy and Dingwall (2003).
24. James ([1907] 1981).
25. *Generalization* may seem to be the wrong way to talk about certain theories, especially those that are developed to explain single cases. However, as we further develop in chapter 5, even a theoretical narrative about a single case relies on variation *within* the case, and on an extrapolation and generalization of such variation. Additionally, single-case theories, explicitly or implicitly, assume that some aspects of the narrative would be useful for understanding other cases—that is, that there is something generalizable about it.
26. Despite the fact that the pragmatist notion of use is future oriented (in its consequences for potential future audiences and problems), this definition is not blind to attempts to account for past occurrences. However, the use of a theory about the *past* would still be in its use for *future* researchers and observations.
27. See Abend (2008).
28. See Tavory and Timmermans (2009).
29. The distinction between descriptive and grammatical theory is heuristic. Most theoretical syntheses make claims that include both descriptive and grammatical elements. Thus, for example, Foucault (e.g., 1964, 1970) makes strong claims about the primacy of discursive formations for understanding the world and claims regarding the specific discursive formations since the early modern period; Bourdieu (1977, 1990) makes claims regarding the generative principles of action and claims regarding the structure of fields in modern France. In general, we find that the more limited the theory to a specific set of problems, the more descriptive it is—see, for example, Merton's (1968) middle-range theories.
30. See also Burawoy (1998).
31. Dewey (1929); James ([1907] 1981).
32. In much the same way, sociologist Andrew Abbott (2004) explores theoretical debates for their heuristic potential; existing theories can be read as multiple possibilities of argumentation, ways of seeing that may foster further theoretical innovation.
33. This argument is hotly debated. This mundane example raises two issues. First, as pragmatists and others have pointed out all along, we always inhabit multiple positions. As G. H. Mead (1934) put it, for every group we belong to, we develop an appreciation of the "generalized other" and of ways that "one should" understand action and occurrences in the world. But the fact that we inhabit multiple publics in different situations means that there are always multiple generalized

others and thus that the specific generalized other we evoke in any given situation is not predetermined. Although we may learn to typify objects and situations in a specific way, we will typify the same object differently in shifting situations. In the graffiti example, we understand the doodle on our wall simultaneously as sociologists, as art connoisseurs, and as residents concerned about real estate prices. We embody multiple positions at once and thus perceive the same object from multiple directions.

Second, the forms and strategies of action available within each of these social worlds are highly complex and provide multiple templates for action—a point that theorists like Mead and Pierre Bourdieu perhaps did not appreciate enough. As sociologists of culture have been stressing over the past few decades, occupying a position means that we learn not simply one specific way of acting and perceiving but multiple patterns of action and meaning through which we solve the puzzles we encounter in our everyday lives. In that sense, it is not only because we simultaneously belong to different social worlds that we can encase the same observation is different ways, but because being part of a social world is to learn to encase the same observation in a number of ways. This insight was captured both by repertoire theorists in the United States (for example, Swidler 1986, 2001) and by the emergent neopragmatism in France, led by Laurent Thevenot and Luc Boltanski (Boltanski and Thevenot 2006; see also Silber 2003).

34. Tavory (2010).
35. Ibid., 61.
36. Gurwitsch (1985).
37. Tavory (2010, 63).
38. Bunn (2010); Hedegard (2013).
39. Blee and McDowell (2012); communication with Blee.
40. See Burawoy (1998); Eliasoph and Lichterman (1999).

Chapter 4

1. Among these books are Charmaz (2006); Clarke (2005); Emerson, Fretz, and Shaw (1995); and Weiss (1994).
2. Festinger (1957); Snyder and Cantor (1979).
3. Snyder and Cantor (1979, 333).
4. Geertz (1973, 30).
5. Strauss (1987).
6. Here we use Corbin and Strauss's (2008) approach to coding.
7. Clarke (2005).
8. The Russian *ostraneniye*, which we are here translating as "defamiliarization," is sometimes translated as "enstrangement." Although the latter is perhaps a better-sounding translation, we decided on "defamiliarization" because "enstrangement" seems to have neo-Marxist connotations of alienation that we wish to avoid; see also Vatulesco (2006).
9. Shklovsky ([1917] 1965).

10. Ibid., 5.

11. Ibid.

12. Vatulesco (2006).

13. The idea of defamiliarization became quite influential in literary studies and beyond. Bertolt Brecht, for example, wrote his plays specifically to produce defamiliarization; see, for example, Brecht (1949, 1961). Brecht's plays manipulated well-known social tropes so viewers would feel "alienated" and come to see the society they live in—and especially capitalism and status hierarchies—through defamiliarized eyes, thus seeing the injuries and injustices hidden by habituation. Bringing this notion into sociology, Peter Berger's (1963) seminal *Invitation to Sociology* argued that the main way in which sociology enriches our understanding of social life is by rendering the familiar strange—by sustaining an attitude of defamiliarization. Jane Addams shared a similar idea in *Democracy and Social Ethics* ([1902] 2002), claiming that her observations at Hull House helped her sustain "perplexity."

14. See Goody (1977).

15. Marion (2002).

16. See Katz (2001b).

17. CP 7.36, 5.183.

18. Vaughan (2004, 2009). The following account is mainly based on Vaughan's various articles and books. However, in order to produce a more granulated picture of the interplay of observations and theorizing, we also interviewed Vaughan about her use of observations.

19. Vaughan (2004, 319).

20. Vaughan (1983).

21. Vaughan (2004, 320).

22. See, for example, Tavory and Eliasoph (2013).

23. For an extreme case of such a process, see the work of Colin Jerolmack (2009, 2013), in which he shows how people can imagine that pigeons come to feed for the sake of friendship. As long as the pigeons come and eat, the people can sustain the narrative.

24. Vaughan (1996).

Chapter 5

1. As Goertz and Mahoney (2012) point out, the basic mathematical logic behind qualitative research is set theory (a theory of collection of objects). However, set-theoretical language is, at best, incomplete. As we show throughout the chapter, qualitative research and theorizing cannot be formalized into mathematical set-propositions.

2. CP 5.402.

3. Misak 2013, 30.

4. There are important differences between James and Peirce, especially if we follow, as we generally do here, Peirce's later formulations of his philosophical project.

One important difference is that whereas Peirce intends his pragmatic maxim to be a definition of meaning surpassing both denotation and connotation, James takes the maxim as a definition of truth. Moreover, whereas for later Peirce consequences include the realm of modal would-bes of subjunctive conditionals, James opts for a more indicative mode. For the matter at hand, however, the squirrel example is useful.

5. James ([1907] 1981); italics in the original.

6. The pragmatic maxim also feeds into Peirce's notion of semiotics. Qualitative research theorizes actors' chains of meaning. And, much as in the pragmatic maxim, actors' meanings are also defined by their effects—that is, not only by the relationship between sign and object, but by their effect in the interpretant. In Peirce's later work, he explicitly fused his semiotics with the pragmatic maxim, trying to prove the veracity of the maxim through his semiotics; see Houser (1998, xxxv–xxxvi).

7. We develop this point further in our discussion of plausibility in chapter 7. In essence, however, we believe that although Peirce's later move to the subjunctive is an important corrective to a theory of truth, it fails as a way to define concepts. We also think that the example given by Peirce (and used by Peirceans) to make the subjunctive point is misleading. In this example we ask about the hardness of a diamond that can never be tested for hardness because it is stuck somewhere we can't get to. In an indicative mood, the answer is that the diamond is neither hard nor soft: if we can't test it, hardness becomes meaningless as part of the definition. In a subjunctive mood, the diamond is still hard, because if we had tried to break it with a hammer it would have been hard. The flaw in this example is that we know what diamonds are through testing probably-similar diamonds that were found to be hard. That the subjunctive is problematic becomes clear if we replace "diamond" with "unknown mineral" in the example. Although the perfect definition would cover all of its subjunctive propositions, at any one point we would not be able to provide such a definition. Thus, in our view, the subjunctive mode is a regulative horizon rather than a guide for theory construction.

8. CP 5.402. By indirect experience, Peirce meant to include not only observable action but also thought. As Peirce scholar Misak (2010, 83) puts it: "Experience is the tribunal against which beliefs are tested, but it does not give us access to a truth unclothed by human cognitive capacities and interests." Indeed, the qualification of indirect effects matters. Peirce argued that mathematical or formal statements can also be subjected to verification because one can manipulate proofs and models and observe the results.

9. As Misak (1991) argues, Peirce does not oppose denotation and connotation but contends that consequences-for-action is a complementary and superior route.

10. See, for example, Anderson (2011); Pager (2007).

11. Lakatos (1976).

12. On the relationship between pragmatism and logical empiricism, see chapter 9 of Misak (2013).

13. See, for example, Becker (1998); Katz (2001a); and Znaniecki (1934).

14. Katz (2001a).
15. Although there may be other ways of addressing variation, we believe that these three forms account for the kinds of variation used in contemporary ethnography. A multisited ethnography (see Marcus 1995), for example, is a combination of dataset variation and intersituational variation; an ethnographic revisit (Burawoy 2003) is a special instance of layering dataset variation and variation over time; a comparative ethnography is no longer a separate kind of ethnography because every ethnography has a comparative component, either internally, based on variation among observations, or by way of research design, when ethnographers are comparing various research sites.
16. Mitchell Duneier (1999) referred to the "extended place method." The issue, however, is not necessarily the movement from place to place, but the tracing of different situations—some of which may occur at the same place, others in different locales.
17. In some sense, all three of the types of variation we describe in this chapter form datasets. *Dataset variation*, however, refers to a set where elements are easily recognized as belonging to the same set, without necessary recourse to social theory (as in intersituational variation).
18. For ideal types, see Weber (2011); for the work of John Stuart Mill on variation, see Mill ([1843] 2002). As the attentive reader can see, the use of variation implies here a search for causal agents and thus also temporality. We will return to causality in the next chapter. As for temporality, we note that although the researcher makes use of temporality in order to reject or accept the relative importance of different characteristics of the observation, the comparison itself is synchronic. In this regard, the temporality of dataset variation and of variation over time crucially diverge.
19. See, for example, Small (2009).
20. See also Goertz and Mahoney (2012).
21. See Hughes (1945); Merton (1976).
22. See, for example, Garfinkel (1967).
23. According to Jack Katz, Howard Becker trained his students to ask respondents a question and then simply follow up with, "And what happened next?"
24. For path dependency, see, for example, Mahoney (2000); for the analytical importance of turning points, see Abbott (1997b); for a summary of "process tracing," see Mahoney (2012). For the narrativity of everyday action, see Tavory and Timmermans (2009) and Tavory and Eliasoph (2013).
25. See Tavory and Eliasoph (2013).
26. Sewell (1996).
27. Ibid., 850.
28. For enjoyment of marijuana smoking, see Becker (1953); for the process of becoming a boxer, see Wacquant (2004); for modeling scouts, see Mears (2012); for opera fanatics, see Benzecry (2009); for religious converts, see Tavory and Winchester (2012).
29. See Blee 2012.

30. There are affinities between our notion of intersituational variation and Mill's ([1843] 2002) notion of "the method of agreement," in which similarities between cases that are different in every other way are compared. However, for Mill the focus here is on the emergence of similar effects, whereas intersituational variation often analyzes various situations in which different effects arise. For Mill, the logic of inclusion of the disparate elements is the common effects of the elements; for us, it is the ability of a theorization to account for different situations on the basis of the similarity of one aspect of meaning-making.

31. Whyte (1943); Liebow (1967); Duneier (1999).

32. See, for example, Bourdieu 1984; Stouffer 1955.

33. Anderson (1999).

34. This is an important part of what made Georg Simmel's formal sociology so powerful. Simmel showed how phenomena that are substantively different in terms of their content are similar enough in terms of their form to merit their inclusion in a shared set (Simmel 1972); see also Zerubavel (1980).

35. Timmermans and Buchbinder (2013).

36. The actual false positive rate would be higher than this number, since many false positives are eliminated before they are referred to the specialty follow-up center (Feuchtbaum, Dowray, and Lorey 2010).

37. Four additional families refused participation, and one family was ineligible for the study because the parents spoke neither English nor Spanish. The ethnographers recorded a total of 193 patient visits, with one to twelve visits recorded per patient. In fourteen of the families, Spanish was the primary language.

38. This was not a random choice. This research project was funded, and the literature on uncertainty was highlighted in the research proposal.

39. Fox (1957).

40. Fox (1980, 2000).

41. Atkinson (1984); Gerrety et al. (1992); Light (1979).

42. Davis (1960); Parsons (1951). Early medical sociologists observed that the uncertainty of medical knowledge complicated communication between health professionals and their patients because of different expectations for the interaction, but that clinical uncertainty could also be used strategically to induce patients to accept medical care.

43. Atkinson (1995).

44. Timmermans and Buchbinder (2010).

45. Timmermans and Buchbinder (2013, 10).

Chapter 6

1. Some theorists attempt to avoid this minefield by separating explanation and causation (Abbott 2001; Martin 2011). Although this is a prudent approach that has some historical justification (because causation was linked to untenable "covering laws"), we think this attempt is bound to fail and that certainly does not sidestep the philosophical problem of causation. If explanation asks why an

event (or set of events) unfolds (see Elster 1989; Martin 2011), it asks about chains of actions that affect other actions. This, as far as we are concerned, is a question about causes and effects. For an alternative approach to causality grounded in pragmatism that focuses on mechanisms, see Gross (2009a).

2. This regularity-based notion of causality is derived from the work of Hume (1967 [1740]); see also Goertz and Mahoney (2012).

3. Dewey (1929, 1938); Whitford (2002).

4. Reiss (2009).

5. Still we are a long way from counterfactual thinking as practiced in the quantitative social sciences (see Morgan and Winship 1997). Our view of counterfactual thinking bears more resemblance to Woodward's (2002) argument that a mechanism-based approach involves counterfactual thinking because every link in the causal chain is counterfactually connected to others. This is true even if the conditions under study are what Mackie (1965) termed "INUS conditions": insufficient elements that are unnecessary (though possible) configurations.

6. See also Hedström and Ylikoski 2010. Note that *mechanism* is used here metaphorically to refer to potentially generalizable processes and goes beyond the narrow connotation of a machine-like regularity. This loose sense also seems to be closer to the way Robert Merton (1968) treated mechanisms in his discussion of the self-fulfilling prophecy, one of the key references for mechanistic accounts in the social sciences.

7. Machamer, Darden, and Craver 2000, 3.

8. See ibid., 13; Stinchcombe 1998, 267.

9. Gross, 2009a, 363.

10. See, for example, Elster 1989; Hedström 2005.

11. For the sociality of reason, see, for example, Bourdieu 1997; Whitford 2002. For the interactional emergence of reason, see Blumer 1969; Garfinkel 1967.

12. Gross (2009a, 368).

13. Ibid, 369; see also Reed (2011).

14. Of course, even such an approach to causality, as Dewey stressed, is a logical "slicing" of a continuously changing and complex world, a temporal stream in which cause and effect may be abstracted but can never be neatly separated (Dewey 1929; 1938; Whitford 2002). A simple C→E form of causal analysis is thus problematic when it leads us to forget that as a continuous stream, events are both unique and unbounded, so that each element pertaining to the event acquires its meaning from its context. In the apt metaphor of philosopher James Bennet (1980, 228), whereas a discrete-event view of causality would lead us to think of the concatenation of cause and effect in a dominoes-like fashion, in which each domino takes down another, in Dewey's view causality is much more like mixing spices in a recipe in which each ingredient partly defines the taste (see also Katz 2012b). And just as spices in a recipe give rise to a particular flavor, the interaction between elements of a situation is consequential for action.

15. Goffman (1974).

16. Ibid., 379.

17. Brown and Zavestoski (2004); Epstein (1996); Karkazis (2008).
18. Karkazis (2008).
19. Geertz (1995, 62).
20. Clinicians would disagree with this assessment: for them, feeding difficulties do not indicate MCADD but would put Michael at higher risk for metabolic complications if he had MCADD.
21. See Mills (1940).
22. Link and Phelan (1995); Lutfey and Freese (2005).
23. Keeley, Wright, and Condit (2009).
24. Green (2007); Landsman (2005); Leiter et al. (2004); Timmermans and Freidin (2007).
25. Irwin and Elley (2011); Lareau (2003).
26. Ricoeur (1984–1988).
27. Halpern (2004).
28. See Paul (1997).
29. For the extensive discourse related to prenatal screening, see Rapp (1998).
30. Such as Diane Paul (1997) and Susan Lindee (2005).
31. See White (1987).

Chapter 7

1. Even though peer review may remain highly problematic and award committees may be systematically biased to reward the "old boys' network," these communities come into being when they discuss, criticize, and comment on research. For the pitfalls of peer review, see Cole, Cole, and Simon (1981); Hirschauer (2010); Travis and Collins (1991); Zuckerman and Merton (1971); for a discussion of the old boys' network, see Cole (1979) and Merton (1973). For a discussion of the academic community, see Lamont (2009).
2. Latour (1987, 78). In Latour's view, science is made through associations between various elements—such as observations and theoretical claims. A trial of strength tests these associations by questioning each of the links the scientist put into place. If the associations hold, the science becomes more objective and factual. If they do not hold, the claims are someone's unsupported opinion and are considered more subjective. Objectivity, credibility, validity, generalizability, causality, and other criteria to evaluate science are relative to the trials research has undergone and have become achieved characteristics.
3. CP 5.372.
4. CP 5.386.
5. The community of inquiry also corrects an overly individualistic reading of the interpretant. Peirce's emphasis on an interpretant's personal attributes cultivated through history, accidents, and experiences may give the impression of scientific individualism. If every configuration that makes up an interpretant is unique, how can science be anything more than an individual semiotic chain? The community of inquiry highlights that such semiotics are profoundly social.

6. CP 5.265; emphasis in original.

7. Thalisse (2004, 25). In his educational writings, John Dewey further emphasized that democratic interactions lie at the basis of communities of inquiry and that multiple communities of inquiry are required to safeguard against insulated expert knowledge. Similarly, Helen Longino (1990), following Habermas, argued that the free exchange of criticism and responsiveness to such criticism form the conditions for the social valuation of science. In a related way, Ludwik Fleck (1979 [1935]) noted that the factuality of research is established through resistance and reinforcement, or social conditioning, of the "thought collective," making scientific truth a historically emergent construction.

8. Thalisse (2004, 25)

9. Sociologists of science since the 1950s have studied the normative and communal character of science on the basis of its reward structure, its referencing practices, and other institutional incentives; see, for example, Merton (1973).

10. Farrell (2001).

11. See also Latour (1987); Sennett (2012).

12. Lichterman and Reed (2012).

13. Although a full discussion goes beyond the scope of our argument, we note that there are important disagreements among the founders of pragmatism on how to balance the pragmatist maxim, the theory of truth, and the community of inquiry (Misak 2010; 2013). With an eye on justifying religious experience and mysticism, William James harnessed pragmatism for what it meant to individual beliefs. His pragmatist approach to religion involved determining not whether God exists, but whether believing in God is useful for individuals. Consequently, James's theory of truth became subject-dependent. Contemporary pragmatists such as Richard Rorty have taken up this relativist strain of pragmatism. Rorty has renounced truth as a goal of inquiry because, he argues, holding justified or true beliefs does not make a difference. His stream of pragmatism puts greater emphasis on the epistemic community as an arbiter of inquiry: whatever one can pass by the community of inquiry counts.

    Most scholars detect a more realist streak in the work of the other founder of pragmatism. Peirce posited that truth was possible—not in an absolute, timeless sense, but in the sense of a community of inquiry investigating as far as it possibly could. As we saw in the discussion of sign-object semiotics, Peirce held that objects limit possible perceptual affordances. In his discussion of abduction, Peirce also argued that concepts and theories should be subjunctively verified with additional inquiry. Thus, the community of inquiry helps constitute truth claims, but not just anything goes. The community's power to adjudicate beliefs is limited by the empirical results and thought experiments of inquiry. The evaluative criteria of qualitative research, then, hinge not on consensus formation but on the challenges to evidence and theoretical inferences.

14. Geertz (1988).

15. Shapin and Schaffer (1985, 60); emphasis in original.

16. Porter (1996).

17. Moller (2000, 47).
18. Ibid., 29–30.
19. Ibid., 32.
20. Klinenberg (2002).
21. Ibid, 127.
22. Duneier (2006).
23. Klinenberg (2006).
24. Garfinkel (1981, 27).
25. Katz (2012a, 1). As we showed in the previous chapter, qualitative researchers are exposed not only to their disciplinary community of inquiry but also to explanations constructed by actors in the field. Researchers' interlocutors have their own explanations about why they act the way they do, and why others act as they do. These explanations matter: Peirce's community of inquiry is inclusive, "with no prior ring-fencing of what counts as the community" (Misak 2013, 37). Still, although scholars need to consider these alternative explanations, they are not beholden to them.
26. Katz (1997).
27. Jansen (2007).
28. Ibid., 988.
29. See Conway (2008) for Ireland, Vaillant (2013) for Uruguay, Agbonifo (2011) for the Niger Delta, and Kim and Fine (2013) for Korea.
30. Quoted in Misak (2013, 34).
31. Ibid., 37.
32. Longino (1990, 79).

Conclusions

1. Steiner ([1956] 1999, 103–7).
2. As Krause (2012) put it, theory should not be considered a subfield, but an anti-subfield, a part of research across substantive topics.
3. Joas (1993).

REFERENCES

Abbott, Andrew. 1997a. "Of Time and Space: The Contemporary Relevance of the Chicago School." *Social Forces* 75 (4): 1149–82.

———. 1997b. "On the Concept of Turning Point." *Comparative Social Research* 16:89–109.

———. 2001. *Time Matters: On Theory and Method.* Chicago: University of Chicago Press.

———. 2004. *Methods of Discovery: Heuristics of the Social Sciences.* New York: Norton.

Abend, Gabriel. 2008. "The Meaning of 'Theory.'" *Sociological Theory* 26:173–99.

Addams, Jane. (1902) 2002. *Democracy and Social Ethics.* Urbana: University of Illinois Press.

Adler, Patricia A., and Peter Adler. 1987. *Membership Roles in Field Research.* Newbury Park, CA: SAGE.

Agbonifo, John. 2011. "Territorialising Niger Delta Conflicts: Place and Contentious Mobilisation." *Interface* 3 (1): 240–65.

Anderson, Douglas R. 2005. "The Esthetic Dimension of Abduction." *Semiotica* 153:9–22.

Anderson, Elijah. 1999. *Code of the Street: Decency, Violence and the Moral Life of the Inner City.* New York: W. W. Norton.

———. 2011. *The Cosmopolitan Canopy: Race and Civility in Everyday Life.* New York: W. W. Norton.

Atkinson, Paul. 1984. "Training for Certainty." *Social Science and Medicine* 19:949–56.

———. 1990. *The Ethnographic Imagination: Textual Constructions of Reality.* New York: Routledge.

———. 1995. *Medical Talk and Medical Work: The Liturgy of the Clinic.* London: SAGE.

Ayim, Maryann. 1974. "Retroduction: The Rational Instinct." *Transactions of the Charles S. Peirce Society* 10 (1): 34–43.

Bacon, Francis. (1620) 1994. *Novum Organum.* 3 vols. Peru, IL: Carus.

Beauvoir, Simone de. 1965. *A Very Easy Death.* New York: Pantheon.

Becker, Howard. S. 1953. "Becoming a Marijuana User." *The American Journal of Sociology* 59 (3): 235–42.

———. 1967. "Whose Side Are We On?" *Social Problems* 14:239–47.

————. 1998. *Tricks of the Trade: How to Think about Your Research while You're Doing It.* Chicago: University of Chicago Press.

Becker, Howard S., Blanche Geer, Everett C. Hughes, and Anselm L. Strauss. 1961. *Boys in White: Student Culture in Medical School.* Chicago: University of Chicago Press.

Bennet, James O. 1980. "Dewey and Causality and Novelty." *Transactions of the Charles S. Peirce Society* 16 (3): 225–41.

Benzecry, Claudio. 2009. "Becoming a Fan: On the Seductions of Opera." *Qualitative Sociology* 32 (2): 131–51.

Berger, Peter L. 1963. *Invitation to Sociology: A Humanistic Perspective.* New York: Doubleday.

Berger, Peter L., and Thomas Luckmann. 1966. *The Social Construction of Reality: A Treatise in the Sociology of Knowledge.* New York: Doubleday.

Bhaskar, Roy. 1997. *A Realist Theory of Science.* London, Verso.

————. 1998. *The Possibility of Naturalism: A Philosophical Critique of the Contemporary Human Sciences.* London: Routledge.

Blee, Kathleen. 2012. *Democracy in the Making: How Activist Groups Form.* Oxford: Oxford University Press.

Blee, Kathleen, and Amy McDowell. 2012. "The Duality of Spectacle and Secrecy: A Case Study of Fraternalism in the 1920s US Ku Klux Klan." *Ethnic and Racial Studies* 36 (2): 249–65.

Blumer, Herbert. 1954. "What Is Wrong with Social Theory?" *American Sociological Review* 19 (1): 3–10.

————. 1969. *Symbolic Interactionism: Perspective and Method.* Englewood Cliffs, NJ: Prentice Hall.

Boltanski, Luc, and Laurent Thevenot. 2006. *On Justification: Economies of Worth.* Princeton, NJ: Princeton University Press.

Bourdieu, Pierre. 1977. *Outline of a Theory of Practice.* Cambridge: Cambridge University Press.

————. 1984. *Distinction: A Social Critique of the Judgment of Taste.* London: Routledge.

————. 1990. *The Logic of Practice.* Cambridge: Polity.

————. 1997. *Pascalian Meditations.* Stanford, CA: Stanford University Press.

Bourdieu, Pierre, and Loïc Wacquant. 1992. *An Invitation to Reflexive Sociology.* Chicago: University of Chicago Press.

Braithwaite, Richard B. 1953. *Scientific Explanation.* Cambridge: Cambridge University Press.

Brecht, Bertolt. 1949. "A Model for Epic Theater." *Sewanee Review* 57 (3): 425–36.

————. 1961. "Theatre for Learning." *The Tulane Drama Review* 6 (1): 18–25.

Brewer, John D. 2000. *Ethnography.* Buckingham, UK: Open University Press.

Brown, Phil, and Stephen Zavestoski. 2004. "Social Movements in Health: An Introduction." *Sociology of Health and Illness* 26:679–94.

Brubaker, Rogers. 1993. "Social Theory as Habitus." In *Bourdieu: Critical Perspectives,* edited by C. Calhoun, E. LiPuma, and M. Postone, 214–34. Chicago: University of Chicago Press.

Bryant, Antony, and Kathy Charmaz. 2007. "Grounded Theory in Historical Perspective: An Epistemological Account." In *The SAGE Handbook of Grounded Theory*, edited by Anthony Bryant and Kathy Charmaz, 31–57. Los Angeles: SAGE.

Bunn, Sherilyn. 2010. "Straight Talk: The Implications of Repealing Don't Ask, Don't Tell and the Rationale for Preserving Aspects of the Current Policy." *Military Review* 203:207–84.

Burawoy, Michael. 1991. *Ethnography Unbound: Power and Resistance in the Modern Metropolis*. Berkeley: University of California Press.

———. 1998. "The Extended Case Method." *Sociological Theory* 16:4–34.

———. 2000. *Global Ethnography: Forces, Connections and Imaginations in a Postmodern World*. Berkeley: University of California Press.

———. 2003. "Revisits: An Outline of a Theory of Reflexive Ethnography." *American Sociological Review* 68:645–79.

Caplow, Theodore. 1984. "Rule Enforcement without Visible Means: Christmas Gift Giving in Middletown." *American Journal of Sociology* 89 (6): 1306–23.

Chalmers, Ian. 1999. *What Is This Thing Called Science?* 3rd rev. ed. St. Lucia: University of Queensland Press.

Charmaz, Kathy. 2000. "Grounded Theory: Objectivist and Constructivist Methods." In *Handbook of Qualitative Research*, edited by Norman K. Denzin and Yvonna S. Lincoln, 509–35. Thousand Oaks, CA: SAGE.

———. 2006. *Constructing Grounded Theory: A Practical Guide through Qualitative Analysis*. Thousand Oaks, CA: SAGE.

———. 2009. "Shifting the Grounds: Constructivist Grounded Theory Methods." In *Developing Grounded Theory: The Second Generation*, edited by Janice M. Morse, Phyllis Noerager Stern, Juliet Corbin, Barbara Bowers, Kathy Charmaz and Adele Clarke. Walnut Creek, CA: Left Coast Press.

Clarke, Adele. 2005. *Situational Analysis: Grounded Theory after the Postmodern Turn*. Thousand Oaks, CA: SAGE.

———. 2009. "From Grounded Theory to Situational Analysis: What's New? Why? How." In *Developing Grounded Theory*, edited by Jan Morse, Phylis N. Stern, Juliet Corbin, Barbara Bowers, Kathy Charmaz and Adele Clarke. Walnut Creek, CA: Left Coast Press.

Coffey, Amanda, Beverley Holbrook, and Paul Atkinson. 1996. "Qualitative Data Analysis: Technologies and Representations." *Sociological Research Online* 1, no. 1, http://www.socresonline.org.uk/1/1/4.html.

Cole, Stephen. 1979. "Age and Scientific Performance." *American Journal of Sociology* 84 (4): 958–77.

Cole, Stephen, Jonathan R. Cole, and Gary A. Simon. 1981. "Chance and Consensus in Peer-Review." *Science* 214 (4523): 881–86.

Collins, Harry. 1985. *Changing Order: Replication and Induction in Scientific Practice*. London: SAGE.

Collins, Patricia Hill. 1992. "Transforming the Inner Circle: Dorothy Smith's Challenge to Sociological Theory." *Sociological Theory* 10:73–80.

Conway, Brian. 2008. "Local Conditions, Global Environment and Transnational

Discourses in Memory Work: The Case of Bloody Sunday (1972)." *Memory Studies* 1 (2): 187–209.

Corbin, Juliet, and Anselm L. Strauss. 2008. *Basics of Qualitative Research*. 3rd ed. Thousand Oaks, CA: SAGE.

Culyba, Rebbecca. J., Carol A. Heimer, and JuLeigh C. Petty. 2004. "The Ethnographic Turn: Fact, Fashion or Fiction." *Qualitative Sociology* 27 (4): 365–89.

Davis, Fred. 1960. "Uncertainty in Medical Prognosis, Clinical and Functional." *American Journal of Sociology* 66:41–47.

———. 1961. "Deviance Disavowal: The Management of Strained Interaction by the Visibly Handicapped." *Social Problems* 9:120–32.

———. 1963. *Passage through Crisis: Polio Victims and Their Families*. New Brunswick, NJ: Bobbs-Merrill.

Denzin, Norman K. 2001. *Interpretive Interactionism*. Thousand Oaks, CA: SAGE.

Denzin, Norman K., and Yvonna S. Lincoln. 1994. *Handbook of Qualitative Research*. Thousand Oaks, CA: SAGE.

Dewey, John. 1929. *Experience and Nature*. LaSalle, IL: Open Court Publishing.

———. 1938. *Logic: The Theory of Inquiry*. New York: Henry Holt.

Dey, Ian. 1999. *Grounding Grounded Theory*. San Diego: Academic Press.

Dreyfus, Hubert L. 1991. *Being-in-the-World: A Commentary on Heidegger's Being and Time, Division I*. Cambridge, MA.: MIT University Press.

Duneier, Mitchell. 1999. *Sidewalk*. New York: Farrar, Straus and Giroux.

———. 2004. "Scrutinizing the Heat: On Ethnic Myths and the Importance of Shoe Leather." *Contemporary Sociology* 33 (2): 139–50.

———. 2006. "The Ecological Fallacy and the 1995 Heat Wave." *American Sociolgical Review* 71 (4): 679–88.

Eliasoph, Nina, and Paul Lichterman. 1999. "'We Begin with Our Favorite Theory . . .': Reconstructing the Extended Case Method." *Sociological Theory* 17:228–334.

Ellis, Carolyn. 1995. *Final Negotiations: A Story of Love, Loss, and Chronic Illness*. Philadelphia: Temple University Press.

Elster, Jon. 1989. *Nuts and Bolts for the Social Sciences*. Cambridge: Cambridge University Press.

Emerson, Robert M., Rachel I. Fretz, and Linda L. Shaw. 1995. *Writing Ethnographic Fieldnotes*. Chicago: University of Chicago Press.

Epstein, Steven. 1996. *Impure Science: AIDS, Activism, and the Politics of Knowledge*. Berkeley: University of California Press.

Fann, K. T. 1970. *Peirce's Theory of Abduction*. The Hague: Martinus Nijhoff.

Farrell, Michael. 2001. *Collaborative Circles: Friendship Dynamics and Creative Work*. Chicago: University of Chicago Press.

Faunce, W. A., and R. L. Fulton. 1958. "The Sociology of Death: A Neglected Area of Research?" *Social Forces* 36:205–9.

Festinger, Leon. 1957. *A Theory of Cognitive Dissonance*. Stanford, CA: Stanford University Press.

Feuchtbaum, Lisa, Sunaina Dowray, and Fred Lorey. 2010. "The Context and Approach for the California Newborn Screening Short- and Long-Term Follow-Up Data System: Preliminary Findings." *Genetics in Medicine* 12:S242–50.

Fine, Gary Alan. 1995. *A Second Chicago School? The Development of a Postwar American Sociology*. Chicago: University of Chicago Press.

Fleck, Ludwik. 1981. *Genesis and Development of a Scientific Fact*. Chicago: University of Chicago Press.

Foucault, Michel. 1964. *Madness and Civilization: A History of Insanity in the Age of Reason*. New York: Pantheon.

———. 1970. *The Order of Things: An Archaeology of the Human Sciences*. New York: Random House.

Fox, Renee C. 1957. "Training for Uncertainty." In *The Student Physician*, edited by R. K. Merton, G. Reader, and P. L. Kendall, 207–41. Cambridge, MA: Harvard University Press.

———. 1980. "The Evolution of Medical Uncertainty." *Milbank Memorial Fund Quarterly* 58:1–49.

———. 2000. "Medical Uncertainty Revisited." In *The Handbook of Social Studies in Health and Medicine*, edited by G. L. Albrecht, R. Fitzpatrick, and S. C. Scrimshaw, 409–25. London: SAGE.

Galison, Peter. 1987. *How Experiments End*. Chicago: University of Chicago Press.

Gallie, Walter B. 1952. *Peirce and Pragmatism*. Harmondsworth: Penguin.

Garfinkel, Alan. 1981. *Forms of Explanation: Rethinking the Questions in Social Theory*. New Haven, CT: Yale University Press.

Garfinkel, Harold. 1967. *Studies in Ethnomethodology*. Oxford: Blackwell.

Geertz, Clifford. 1973. *The Interpretation of Cultures*. New York: Basic Books.

———. 1988. *Works and Lives: The Anthropologist as Author*. Stanford, CA: Stanford University Press.

———. 1995. *After the Fact: Two Countries, Four Decades, One Anthropologist*. Cambridge, MA: Harvard University Press.

Gerrety, Martha S., Jo Anne L. Earp, Robert F. DeVellis, and Donald W. Light. 1992. "Uncertainty and Professional Work: Perceptions of Physicians in Clinical Practice." *American Journal of Sociology* 97 (4): 1022–51.

Gibson, James J. 1979. *The Ecological Approach to Visual Perception*. Boston: Houghton Mifflin.

Glaser, Barney. 1978. *Theoretical Sensitivity*. San Francisco: Sociology Press.

———. 1992a. *Basic of Grounded Theory Analysis*. Mill Valley, CA: Sociology Press.

———. 1992b. *Emergence versus Forcing: Basics of Grounded Theory Research*. Mill Valley, CA: Sociology Press.

———. 2001. *The Grounded Theory Perspective: Conceptualization Contrasted with Description*. Mill Valley, CA: Sociology Press.

———. 2002. "Constructivist Grounded Theory?" *Forum: Qualitative Sozialforschung/ Forum: Qualitative Social Research* 3, no. 3, http://www.qualitative-research.net /index.php/fqs/article/view/825.

Glaser, Barney G., and Anselm L. Strauss. 1965. *Awareness of Dying*. Chicago: Aldine.

————. 1967. *The Discovery of Grounded Theory*. New York: Aldine.

————. 1968. *Time for Dying*. Chicago: Aldine.

Gluckman, Max. (1961) 2006. "Ethnographic Data in British Social Anthropology." In *The Manchester School: Practice and Ethnographic Praxis in Anthropology*, edited by T. M. S. Evens and Don Handelman, 13–22. New York: Berghahn.

Goertz, Gary, and James Mahoney. 2012. *A Tale of Two Cultures: Qualitative and Quantitative Research in the Social Sciences*. Princeton, NJ: Princeton University Press.

Goffman, Erving. 1961. *Asylums: Essays on the Social Situation of Mental Patients and Other Inmates*. New York: Doubleday.

————. 1974. *Frame Analysis: An Essay on the Organization of Experience*. Cambridge, MA: Harvard University Press.

Goody, Jack. 1977. *The Domestication of the Savage Mind*. Cambridge: Cambridge University Press.

Green, Sara E. 2007. "We're Tired, Not Sad": Benefits and Burdens of Mothering a Child with a Disability." *Social Science and Medicine* 64 (1): 150–63.

Gross, Neil. 2009a. "A Pragmatist Theory of Social Mechanisms." *American Sociological Review* 74:358–79.

————. 2009b. *Richard Rorty: The Making of an American Philosopher*. Chicago: University of Chicago Press.

Gurwitsch, Aron. 1985. *Marginal Consciousness*. Athens: Ohio University Press.

Halpern, Sydney A. 2004. *Lesser Harms: The Morality of Risk in Medical Research*. Chicago: University of Chicago Press.

Hammersley, Martyn. 1992. *What's Wrong with Ethnography?* London: Routledge.

Hammersley, Martyn, and Paul Atkinson. 1983. *Ethnography: Principles in Practice*. London: Tavistock.

Hartshorne, Charles, Paul Weiss, and Arthur Burks. 1931–1958. *Collected Papers of Charles Sanders Peirce*. 8 vols. Cambridge, MA: Harvard University Press.

Hedegard, Danielle. 2013. "Blackness and Experience in Omnivorous Cultural Consumption: Evidence from the Tourism of Capoeira in Salvador, Brazil." *Poetics* 41 (1): 1–26.

Hedström, Peter. 2005. *Dissecting the Social: On the Principles of Analytical Sociology*. Cambridge: Cambridge University Press.

Hedström, Peter, and Petri Ylikoski. 2010. "Causal Mechanisms in the Social Sciences." *Annual Review of Sociology* 36:49–67.

Heidegger, Martin. (1927) 1996. *Being and Time*, trans. J. Stambaugh. Albany: SUNY Press.

Hirschauer, Stefan. 2010. "Editorial Judgments: A Praxeology of 'Voting' in Peer Review." *Social Studies of Science* 40 (1): 71–103.

Hood, Jane. 2007. "Orthodoxy vs. Power: The Defining Traits of Grounded Theory." In *Handbook of Grounded Theory*, edited by Anthony Bryant and Kathy Charmaz, 151–64. London: SAGE.

Houser, Nathan. 1998. "Introduction." In Charles S. Peirce, *The Essential Peirce*, 2:xvii–xxxviii. Bloomington: Indiana University Press.

Hughes, Everett C. 1945. "Dilemmas and Contradictions of Status." *American Journal of Sociology* 50:353–59.

Hume, David. (1740) 1966. *A Treatise of Human Nature.* Oxford: Oxford University Press.

Husserl, Edmund. 1960. *Cartesian Meditations: An Introduction to Phenomenology.* The Hague: Martinus Nijhoff.

Irwin, Sarah, and Sharon Elley. 2011. "Concerted Cultivation? Parenting Values, Education and Class Diversity." *Sociology* 45 (3): 480–95.

James, William. 1890. *The Principles of Psychology.* New York: Henry Holt and Company.

———. (1907) 1981. *Pragmatism.* Cambridge, MA: Hackett.

Jansen, Robert. 2007. "Resurrection and Appropriation: Reputational Trajectories, Memory Work and the Political Use of Historical Figures." *American Journal of Sociology* 112 (4): 953–1007.

Jerolmack, Colin. 2009. "Humans, Animals, and Play: Theorizing Interaction When Intersubjectivity Is Problematic." *Sociological Theory* 27: 371–89.

———. 2013. *The Global Pigeon.* Chicago: University of Chicago Press.

Joas, Hans. 1993. *Pragmatism and Social Theory.* Chicago: University of Chicago Press.

———. 1996. *The Creativity of Action.* Chicago: University of Chicago Press.

Karkazis, Katrina. 2008. *Fixing Sex: Intersex, Medical Authority, and Lived Experience.* Durham, NC: Duke University Press.

Katz, Jack. 1997. "Ethnography's Warrants." *Sociological Methods and Research* 25(4): 391–423.

———. 2001a. "Analytical Induction." In *International Encyclopedia of the Social and Behavioral Sciences*, edited by N. J. Smelser and P. B. Baltes, 1:480–84. Oxford: Elsevier.

———. 2001b. "From How to Why: On Luminous Description and Causal Inference in Ethnography (Part 1)." *Ethnography* 2:443–73.

———. 2012a. "Cooks Cooking up Recipes: The Cash Value of Nouns, Verbs and Grammar." *American Sociologist* 43 (1): 125–34.

———. 2012b. "Ethnography for Uncle Max." Paper presented at the *American Journal of Sociology* Conference on Causal Thinking and Ethnographic Research, Chicago, March.

Keeley, Bethany, Lanelle Wright, and Celeste M. Condit. 2009. "Functions of Health Fatalism: Fatalistic Talk as Face Saving, Uncertainty Management, Stress Relief, and Sense Making." *Sociology of Health and Illness* 31 (5): 734–47.

Kelle, Udo. 2007. "The Development of Categories: Different Approaches in Grounded Theory." In *The SAGE Handbook of Grounded Theory*, edited by Anthony Bryant and Kathy Charmaz, 191–214. Los Angeles: SAGE.

Kim, Jeong-Chul, and Gary A. Fine. 2013. "Collaborators and National Memory: The Creation of the Encyclopedia of Pro-Japanese Collaborators in Korea." *Memory Studies* 6 (2): 130–45.

Klinenberg, Eric. 2002. *Heat Wave: A Social Autopsy of Disaster in Chicago.* Chicago: University of Chicago Press.

———. 2006. "Blaming the Victim: Hearsay, Labeling and the Hazards of Quick-Hit Disaster Ethnography." *American Sociological Review* 71 (4): 689–98.

Kordig, Carl R. 1978. "Discovery and Justification." *Philosophy of Science* 45 (1): 110–17.

Krause, Monika. 2012. "Theory as an Anti-Subfield Subfield." *Perspectives: Newsletter of the ASA Theory Section* 34 (2): 6–9.

Kübler-Ross, Elisabeth. 1969. *On Death and Dying*. New York: Macmillan.

Kuhn, Thomas. 1962. *The Structure of Scientific Revolutions*. Chicago: University of Chicago Press.

Lakatos, Imre. 1970. "Falsification and the Methodology of Scientific Research Programmes." In *Criticism and the Growth of Knowledge*, edited by I. Lakatos and A. Musgrave, 91–195. Cambridge: Cambridge University Press.

———. 1976. *Proofs and Refutations: The Logic of Mathematical Discovery*. Cambridge: Cambridge University Press.

Lamont, Michele. 2009. *How Professors Think: Inside the Curious World of Academic Judgment*. Cambridge, MA: Harvard University Press.

Lamont, Michele, and Patricia White. 2005. *Workshop on Interdisciplinary Standards for Systematic Qualitative Research*. Washington, DC: National Science Foundation.

Landsman, Gail. H. 2005. "Mothers and Models of Disability." *Journal of Medical Humanities* 26:121–39.

Lareau, Annette. 2003. *Unequal Childhoods: Class, Race, and Family Life*. Berkeley: University of California Press.

Latour, Bruno. 1987. *Science in Action: How to Follow Scientists and Engineers through Society*. Cambridge, MA: Harvard University Press.

Leiter, Valerie, Marty W. Krauss, Betsy Anderson, and Nora Wells. 2004. "The Consequences of Caring: Effects of Mothering a Child with Special Needs." *Journal of Family Issues* 25 (3): 379–403.

Lichterman, Paul, and Isaac Reed. 2012. "Interpretation and Explanation in Ethnography: A Pragmatist Approach." Paper presented at the American Journal of Sociology Conference on Causal Thinking and Ethnographic Research, Chicago, March.

Liebow, Elliott. 1967. *Tally's Corner: A Study of Negro Streetcorner Men*. Boston, MA: Little, Brown, and Company.

Light, Donald W. 1979. "Uncertainty and Control in Professional Training." *Journal of Health and Social Behavior* 20 (4): 310–22.

Lindee, Susan M. 2005. *Moments of Truth in Genetic Medicine*. Baltimore, MD: Johns Hopkins University Press.

Link, Bruce, and Jo Phelan. 1995. "Social Conditions as Fundamental Causes of Disease." *Journal of Health and Social Behavior* 35:80–94.

Liszka, James J. 1996. *A General Introduction to the Semiotic of Charles Sanders Peirce*. Bloomington: Indiana University Press.

Locke, Karen, Karen Golden-Biddle, and Martha S. Feldman. 2008. "Making Doubt Generative: Rethinking the Role of Doubt in the Research Process." *Organization Science* 19:907–18.

Longino, Helen. 1990. *Science as Social Knowledge: Values and Objectivity in Scientific Inquiry*. Princeton, NJ: Princeton University Press.

Lutfey, Karen, and Jeremy Freese. 2005. "Toward Some Fundamentals of Fundamental Causality: Socioeconomic Status and Health in the Routine Clinic Visit for Diabetes." *American Journal of Sociology* 110 (5): 1326–72.

Macbeth, Douglas. 2001. "On Reflexivity in Qualitative Research: Two Readings and a Third." *Qualitative Inquiry* 7:35–68.

Machamer, Peter, Darden, Lindley and Carl F. Craver. 2000. "Thinking about Mechanisms." *Philosophy of Science* 67 (1): 1–25.

Mackie, John L. 1965. "Clauses and Conditions." *American Philosophical Quarterly* 2:245–64.

MacMillan, Katie, and Thomas Koenig. 2004. "The Wow Factor: Preconceptions and Expectations for Data Analysis Software in Qualitative Research." *Social Science Computer Review* 22 (2): 179–86.

Mahoney, James. 2000. "Path Dependence in Historical Sociology," *Theory and Society* 29 (4): 507–48.

———. 2012. "The Logic of Process Tracing Tests in the Social Sciences." *Sociological Methods and Research* 41 (4): 570–97.

Marcus, George E. 1995. "Ethnography in/of the World System: The Emergence of Multi-Sited Ethnography." *Annual Review of Anthropology* 24:95–117.

Marcus, George E., and Michael M. J. Fischer. 1986. *Anthropology as Cultural Critique: An Experimental Moment in the Human Sciences*. Chicago: University of Chicago Press.

Marion, Jean-Luc. 2002. *In Excess: Studies of Saturated Phenomena*. New York: Fordham University Press.

Martin, John Levi. 2011. *The Explanation of Social Action*. Oxford: Oxford University Press.

McKaughan, Daniel J. 2008. "From Ugly Ducking to Swan: C. S. Peirce, Abduction, and the Pursuit of Scientific Theories." *Transactions of the Charles S. Peirce Society* 44 (3): 446–68.

Mead, George H. 1934. *Mind, Self and Society: From the Standpoint of a Social Behaviorist*. Chicago: Chicago University Press.

Mears, Ashley. 2012. "Tracking Down Culture in a Cultural Economy." Paper presented at the Measuring Culture miniconference, Vancouver, Canada, October.

Merton, Robert K. 1968. *Social Theory and Social Structure*. New York: Free Press.

———. 1973. *The Sociology of Science: Theoretical and Empirical Investigations*, edited by Robert K. Merton. Chicago: University of Chicago Press.

———. 1976. *Sociological Ambivalence and Other Essays*. New York: Free Press.

Merton, Robert K., and Elinor Barber. 2006. *The Travels and Adventures of Serendipity: A Study in Sociological Semantics and the Sociology of Science*. Princeton, NJ: Princeton University Press.

Mill, John S. (1843) 2002. *A System of Logic: Ratiocinative and Inductive*. Honolulu, HI: University Press of the Pacific.

Mills, C. Wright. 1940. "Situated Actions and Vocabularies of Motive." *American Sociological Review* 5 (6): 904–13.

Misak, Cheryl J. 1991. *Truth and the End of Inquiry: A Peircean Account of Truth*. Oxford: Oxford University Press.

———. 2010. "The Pragmatist Maxim: How to Get Leverage on a Concept." *Harvard Review of Philosophy* 17:76–87.

———. 2013. *The American Pragmatists*. Oxford: Oxford University Press.

Mitchell, J. Clyde. 1956. *The Yao Village*. Manchester, UK: Manchester University Press for Rhodes-Livingstone Institute.

Moller, David Wendell. 2000. *Life's End: Technocratic Dying in an Age of Spiritual Yearning*. Amityville, NY: Baywood.

Morgan, Stanley L., and Christopher Winship. 2007. *Counterfactuals and Causal Inference: Methods and Principles for Social Research*. Cambridge, MA: Harvard University Press.

Morris, Charles W. 1946. *Signs, Language and Behavior*. New York: Prentice Hall.

Morse, Janice M. 2009. "Tussles, Tensions, And Resolutions." In *Developing Grounded Theory: The Second Generation*, edited by Janice M. Morse, Noerager Phyllis Stern, Juliet Corbin, Barbara Bowers, Kathy Charmaz, and Adele Clarke. Walnut Creek, CA: Left Coast Press.

Murphy, Elizabeth, and Robert Dingwall. 2003. *Qualitative Methods and Health Policy Research*. New York: Aldine de Gruyter.

Newman, Katherine S. 1999. *No Shame in My Game*. New York: Vintage/Russell Sage Foundation Books.

Obeyesekere, Gananath. 1992. *The Apotheosis of Captain Cook*. Princeton, NJ: Princeton University Press.

Paavola, Sami. 2005. "Peircean Abduction: Instinct, or Inference?" *Semiotica* 153:131–54.

Pager, Devah. 2007. *Marked: Race, Crime and Finding Work in an Era of Mass Incarceration*. Chicago: University of Chicago Press.

Parsons, Talcott. 1951. *The Social System*. Glencoe, IL: The Free Press.

Paul, Diane B. 1997. "The History of Newborn Phenylketonuria Screening in the US." In *Promoting Safe and Effective Genetic Testing in the United States: Final Report of the Taskforce on Genetic Testing*, edited by N. A. Holtzman and M. S. Watson, 137–60. Bethesda, MD: National Institutes of Health.

Peirce, Charles S. (1903) 1997. *Pragmatism as a Principle and Method of Right Thinking: The 1903 Harvard Lectures on Pragmatism*. Albany, NY: SUNY Press.

———. 1992–98. *The Essential Peirce*, edited by Nathan Houser, Christian Kloesel, and the Peirce Edition Project. 2 vols. Bloomington: Indiana University Press.

Popper, Karl. 1959. *The Logic of Scientific Discovery*. New York: Harper.

Porter, Theodore. 1996. *Trust in Numbers: The Pursuit of Objectivity in Science and Public Life*. Princeton, NJ: Princeton University Press.

Ragin, Charles C., Joane Nagel, and Patricia White. 2004. *Workshop on Scientific Foundations of Qualitative Research*. Washington, DC: National Science Foundation.

Rapp, Rayna. 1998. *Testing Women, Testing the Fetus: The Social Impact of Amniocentesis in America*. New York: Routledge.

Reed, Isaac A. 2011. *Interpretation and Social Knowledge: On the Use of Theory in the Human Sciences*. Chicago: University of Chicago Press.

Reichenbach, Hans. 1938. *Experience and Prediction*. Chicago: University of Chicago Press.

Reiss, Julian. 2009. "Causation in the Social Sciences: Evidence, Inference, and Purpose." *Philosophy of the Social Sciences* 39 (1): 20–40.

Rescher, Nicholas. 1978. *Peirce's Philosophy of Science: Critical Studies in His Theory of Induction and Scientific Method*. Notre Dame, IN: University of Notre Dame Press.

Ricoeur, Paul. 1984–88. *Time and Narrative* (three volumes). Chicago: University of Chicago Press.

Robertson, Jennifer. 2002. "Reflexivity Redux: A Pithy Polemic on 'Positionality.'" *Anthropological Quarterly* 75:785–92.

Roth, Julius. 1963. *Timetables: Structuring the Passage of Time in Hospital Treatment and Other Careers*. Indianapolis: Bobbs-Merrill.

Sahlins, Marshall. 1981. *Historical Metaphors and Mythical Realities: Structure in the Early History of the Sandwich Islands Kingdom*. Ann Arbor: University of Michigan Press.

———. 1995. *How Natives Think: About Captain Cook, for Example*. Chicago: University of Chicago Press.

Saussure, Ferdinand de. (1916) 1986. *Course in General Linguistics*. New York: Open Court.

Schutz, Alfred. 1967. *The Phenomenology of the Social World*. Evanston, IL: Northwestern University Press.

Sellars, Wilfrid. (1956) 1997. *Empiricism and the Philosophy of Mind*, edited by Robert Brandom. Cambridge, MA: Harvard University Press.

Sennett, Richard. 2012. *Together: The Rituals, Pleasures and Politics of Cooperation*. New Haven, CT: Yale University Press.

Sewell, William H., Jr. 1996. "Historical Events as Transformations of Structures: Inventing the Revolution at the Bastille." *Theory and Society* 25 (6): 841–81.

Shapin, Steven, and Simon Schaffer. 1985. *Leviathan and the Air-Pump*. Princeton, NJ: Princeton University Press.

Shklovsky, Victor. (1917) 1965. "Art as Technique." In *Russian Formalist Criticism*, edited by L. T. Lemon and M. Reiss, 3–25. Lincoln: University of Nebraska Press.

Short, Thomas L. 2007. *Peirce's Theory of Signs*. Cambridge: Cambridge University Press.

Silber, Ilana F. 2003. "Pragmatic Sociology as Cultural Sociology: Beyond Repertoire Theory?" *European Journal of Social Theory* 6:427–49.

Silver, Daniel. 2011. "The Moodiness of Action." *Sociological Theory* 29 (2): 199–222.

Simmel, Georg. 1972. *Georg Simmel on Individuality and Social Forms*, edited by Don Levine. Chicago: University of Chicago Press.

Small, Mario L. 2009. "'How Many Cases Do I Need?' On Science and the Logic of Case Selection in Field Based Research." *Ethnography* 10 (1): 5–38.

Smith, Dorothy E. 2005. *Institutional Ethnography: A Sociology for People*. Toronto, Canada: AltaMira.

Snyder, Mark, and Nancy Cantor. 1979. "Testing Hypotheses about Other People: The Use of Historical Knowledge," *Journal of Experimental Social Psychology* 15 (4): 330–42.

Star, S. Leigh. 1989. *Regions of the Mind: Brain Research and the Quest for Scientific Certainty*. Stanford, CA: Stanford University Press.

Steiner, Franz B. (1956) 1999. *Taboo, Truth and Religion*. New York: Berghahn.

Stinchcombe, Arthur L. 1998. "Monopolistic Competition as a Mechanism: Corporations, Universities, and Nation-States in Competitive Fields." In *Social Mechanisms: An Analytical Approach to Social Theory*, edited by Peter Hedström and Richard Swedberg, 267–305. Cambridge: Cambridge University Press.

Stouffer, Samuel A. 1955. *Communism, Conformity and Civil Liberties*. New York: Transaction.

Strauss, Anselm L. 1987. *Qualitative Analysis for Social Scientists*. Cambridge: Cambridge University Press.

———. 1993. *Continual Permutations of Action*. New York: Aldine de Gruyter.

Strauss, Anselm L., and Juliet Corbin. 1990. *Basics of Qualitative Research*. Newbury Park, CA: SAGE.

Strauss, Anselm L., and Barney G. Glaser. 1970. *Anguish*. San Francisco: Sociology Press.

Sudnow, David. 1967. *Passing On: The Social Organization of Dying*. Englewood Cliffs, NJ: Prentice-Hall.

Swedberg, Richard. 2012. "Theorizing in Sociology and Social Science: Turning to the Context of Discovery." *Theory and Society* 41 (1): 1–40.

Swidler, Ann. 1986. "Culture in Action: Symbols and Strategies." *American Sociological Review* 51:273–86.

———. 2001. *Talk of Love: How Culture Matters*. Chicago: University of Chicago Press.

Tavory, Iddo. 2010. "Of Yarmulkes and Categories: Delegating Boundaries and the Phenomenology of Interactional Expectation." *Theory and Society* 39:49–68.

Tavory, Iddo, and Nina Eliasoph. 2013. "Coordinating Futures: Towards a Theory of Anticipation." *American Journal of Sociology* 118 (4): 908–42.

Tavory, Iddo, and Ann Swidler. 2009. "Condom Semiotics: Meaning and Condom Use in Rural Malawi." *American Sociological Review* 74 (2): 171–89.

Tavory, Iddo, and Stefan Timmermans. 2009. "Two Cases of Ethnography: Grounded Theory and the Extended Case Method." *Ethnography* 10:1–21.

Tavory, Iddo, and Daniel Winchester. 2012. "Experiential Careers: The Routinization and De-Routinization of Religious Life." *Theory and Society* 41:351–73.

Thalisse, Robert B. 2004. "Towards a Peircean Politics of Inquiry." *Transactions of the Charles S. Peirce Society* 40 (1): 21–38.

Timmermans, Stefan, and Mara Buchbinder. 2010. "Patients-in-Waiting: Living between Sickness and Health in the Genomics Era." *Journal of Health and Social Behavior* 51 (4): 408–23.

———. 2013. *Saving Babies? The Consequences of Newborn Genetic Screening*. Chicago: University of Chicago Press.

Timmermans, Stefan, and Betina Freidin. 2007. "Caretaking as Articulation Work:

The Effects of Taking up Responsibility for a Child with Asthma on Labor Force Participation." *Social Science and Medicine* 65:1351–64.

Timmermans, Stefan, and Iddo Tavory. 2007. "Advancing Ethnographic Research through Grounded Theory Practice." In *Handbook of Grounded Theory*, edited by Anthony Bryant and Kathy Charmaz, 493–513. London: SAGE.

———. 2012. "Theory Construction in Qualitative Research: From Grounded Theory to Abductive Analysis." *Sociological Theory* 30 (3): 167–86.

Titscher, S., M. Meyer, R. Wodak, and E. Vetter. 2000. *Methods of Text and Discourse Analysis*. Thousand Oaks, CA: SAGE.

Tolstoy, Leo. 1960. *The Death of Ivan Illych*. New York: Penguin.

Travis, G. D. L., and H. M. Collins. 1991. "New Light on Old Boys—Cognitive and Institutional Particularism in the Peer-Review System." *Science, Technology, and Human Values* 16 (3): 322–41.

Vaillant, Gabriela G. 2013. "The Politics of Temporality: An Analysis of Leftist Youth Politics and Generational Contention." *Social Movement Studies* 12 (4): 377–96.

van Velsen, Jaap. 1967. "The Extended-Case Method and Situational Analysis." In *The Craft of Social Anthropology*, edited by A. L. Epstein, 153–80. London: Tavistock.

Vatulesco, Christina. 2006. "The Politics of Estrangement: Tracking Shklovsky's Device through Literary and Policing Practices." *Poetics Today* 27 (1): 35–66.

Vaughan, Diane. 1983. *Controlling Unlawful Organizational Behavior*. Chicago: University of Chicago Press.

———. 1996. *The Challenger Launch Decision: Risky Technology, Culture and Deviance at NASA*. Chicago: University of Chicago Press.

———. 2004. "Theorizing Disaster: Analogy, Historical Ethnography, and the Challenger Accident." *Ethnography* 5:315–47.

———. 2009. "Ethnographic Analytics." In *The Oxford Handbook of Analytical Sociology*, edited by Peter Hedström and Peter Bearman, 688–711. Oxford: Oxford University Press.

Wacquant, Loïc. 2002. "Scrutinizing the Street: Poverty, Morality, and the Pitfalls of Urban Ethnography." *American Journal of Sociology* 107 (6): 1468–532.

———. 2004. *Body and Soul: Ethnographic Notebooks of an Apprentice Boxer*. Oxford: Oxford University Press.

Weber, Max. 2011. *Methodology of Social Sciences*, translated and edited by Edward A. Shils and Henry A. Finch. New York: Transaction.

Weiss, Robert S. 1994. *Learning from Strangers: The Art and Method of Qualitative Interview Studies*. New York: Free Press.

White, Hayden. 1987. *The Content of the Form: Narrative Discourse and Historical Representation*. Baltimore, MD: Johns Hopkins University Press.

Whitford, Josh. 2002. "Pragmatism and the Untenable Dualism of Means and Ends: Why Rational Choice Theory Does Not Deserve Paradigmatic Privilege." *Theory and Society* 31:325–63.

Whyte, William F. 1943. *Street Corner Society: The Social Structure of an Italian Slum*. Chicago: University of Chicago Press.

Winship, Christopher. 2006. "Policy Analysis as Puzzle Solving." In *Oxford Handbook of Public Policy*, edited by M. Moran, R. E. Goodin, and M. Rein, 109–23. Oxford: Oxford University Press.

Woodward, Jim. 2002. "What Is a Mechanism? A Counterfactual Account." *Philosophy of Science* 69 (23): S366–S377.

Zerubavel, Eviatar. 1980. "If Simmel Were a Fieldworker: On Formal Sociological Theory and Analytical Field Research." *Symbolic Interaction* 3 (2): 25–34.

Znaniecki, Florian. 1934. *The Method of Sociology*. New York: Farrar & Rinehart.

Zuckerman, Harriet, and Robert K. Merton. 1971. "Patterns of Evaluation in Science: Institutionalisation, Structure and Functions of the Referee System." *Minerva* 9 (1): 66–100.

INDEX

Abbott, Andrew, 140n32

abduction: and causality, 87; culling alternatives, 111–12; definition, 36; double-fitting observations and theory, 84; in everyday life, 38–39; hunches, 111; innovative potential, 38; as insight, 39; logic of, 35–39; and method, 51–66; and multiple theories, 35–49; potential, 79; as process of conjecture, 40; proto-theoretical, 42; relationship to induction and deduction, 5; in scientific research, 37; step in methodology, 38; string of moments, 128; syllogism of, 37–38; uncertainty of, 38

abductive analysis, 121–28; crafting inference, 48; in ethnographic study, 80; inspiration for, 43; maximizing, 61; origins of insights, 39–42; overview of, 122–26; production of inferences in class presentations, 110; recursive nature of, 85; research context, 4–6; search for variation, 71; synopsis of, 131–32

actions, 76–79. *See also* habits of thought and action

actor-network theory, 15, 42–43, 133n10

actors: causal understanding of circumstances, 94; interpretations, 100

Addams, Jane, 142n13

Allport, Gordon, 52

American Journal of Sociology, 135n2

American Sociological Review, 135n2

anthropology, 126–27; poststructuralist, 17. *See also* extended case method

anti-Semitism, 45–49

apperceptions, 139n19

appresentations, 139n19

art, theory of, 56, 59

assumptions, theoretical, 113

authority, and claims of fit, 106

axial coding, 54

Bacon, Francis, 14

Basics of Qualitative Research (Strauss and Corbin), 12

Bastille, storming of, 76–78

Becker, Howard, 144n23

beginnings, 58, 98–99

beliefs, 104–5, 119

Bennet, James, 146n14

Berger, Peter, 11, 142n13

Blau, Peter, 13

Blee, Kathleen, 48

Blumer, Herbert, 10, 15, 137n7

Body and Soul (Wacquant), 133n8

bottoming-out components, 89

Bourdieu, Pierre, 47, 141n33

brainstorming, 9, 27, 53

Brecht, Bertolt, 142n13

Buchbinder, Mara, 80–85

Burawoy, Michael, 18–19, 49

Capital (Marx), 135n2

cases, intensive study of, 127. *See also* extended case method

categories, activation of, 46–47

causal explanations, beginning of, 101

causal extensions, 100